CHANGE YOUR LIFE

Change Your Life

THE POWER OF A FOCUSED MIND

Sandra Forrester

LIONCREST
PUBLISHING

CHANGE YOUR LIFE
The Power of a Focused Mind

FIRST EDITION

ISBN 978-1-5445-3896-9 *Paperback*
978-1-5445-3895-2 *Ebook*
978-1-5445-3973-7 *Audiobook*

Contents

Introduction

Imagine meeting people for the first time and they already know who you are. Not because you're famous or you've invented something that saved lives, but because you found a book in a junk shop, paid fifty cents for it, read it three times in one day, took action, and significantly changed your life.

It happens to me all the time. I don't know why my story is still memorable ten years after I told it at a business convention, because there's nothing special about me. A random set of circumstances set things in motion in a way that continually amazes people.

Here's an example:

Last week, I rang someone within my company, Barfoot & Thompson, which is New Zealand's largest privately owned and arguably most successful real estate company, and said, "Hi. I'm Sandra Forrester from Barfoot & Thompson, and I need to ask you a question about an agreement."

"Sandra Forrester?"

"Yes, that's right."

"Oh, I know you," she said. "You're the person who read the book and became one of the top performers in the company."

I said, "Yes, that's right."

"Wow," she said. "I know exactly who you are."

I can't tell you the number of times I've heard that, not only from real estate agents within my company but from administrators, support people, and others across the business. Yet each time I'm surprised because what I did was such a simple thing. It wasn't complicated and it wasn't expensive.

But it changed my life.

And it can change yours too.

So I have a question for you. Are you stuck at a place where you know things can get better, but you don't know how to transition from where you are to where you want to be, whether that's improving your personal or business life?

Do you feel powerless to change your life?

You're not alone. In fact, it's totally normal and exactly how most people live in this world.

But it doesn't have to be that way.

This is what I now know for sure: the thoughts that you think, the words that you speak, and actions that you take have a huge impact on your life, not only on the present but also on your future. If you can focus and direct them onto specific goals and desires, it creates positive change in that direction, because a focused mind is one of the most powerful forces in the universe.

In this book, you will learn the process to harness and use the power of a focused mind. You will learn that it's possible to reinvent yourself, that you can go from a place of fear and loss and low performance to being one of the top performers in your industry. I'll show you the techniques I've used—techniques that can be used by everyone regardless of age, educational status, occupation, etc.—so that you have a clear formula to obtain success and a vision for how to achieve it.

It doesn't matter what age you are, what you've done in the past, or what is going on in your life right now, you can change your direction.

Author Douglas Lumsden is a great example of someone who took hold of his life and made changes towards a positive future.

He says,

"For what it's worth:

I was forty-three when I got my PhD.

I was fifty-one when I started my dream job.

I was fifty-four when I married the love of my life.

I was fifty-five when I ran my first marathon.

I was sixty-seven when I wrote my first book.

I turn seventy next year, and I can't wait."

And I don't know if you know, but Colonel Sanders didn't start Kentucky Fried Chicken until he was over sixty years old, and he also achieved huge success because he had faith and confidence in what he believed in.

As you can see, it's never too late to start making positive changes in your life.

DO YOU KNOW WHAT YOU WANT?

This may seem a strange thing to say, but most people don't know what they want.

However, they know what they *don't* want.

This too is totally normal.

However, not having a clear purpose or goal keeps you stuck in the day-to-day patterns that is your current life. I would like this book to act like a reset button. To set a foundation for designing a successful and fulfilling life—whatever it is you determine that to be.

I have learnt through my own journey that people become stuck in patterns. Sometimes it's easy and other times it's hard. So when we *don't* know what we want, we aimlessly coast through life. Then one day we wake up and ask, "Is this it? Is this how my life is going to be every day?" If you're asking why you've been stuck in the same cycle for months or years on end, it's because you haven't been aware of or shaken out of these patterns.

There is a theory, and I believe it too, that most people will not enact meaningful change until they reach a state of *fear* or *loss*. If you're overweight, you might try on your size fourteen pants and realise you need a size sixteen now. Or you get a blood test, and your diagnosis comes back as pre-diabetic. Or you have kids and realise you want to live long enough to see them grow up. Only then, after being confronted with these fears and losses, will you lose weight, watch your sugar intake, or start exercising to remain healthy.

This theory proved true for me.

I went from being an average performer earning okay money in real estate to earning nothing for a whole year. My career took a nosedive. I was in a monumental place of fear and loss. It shook me out of my stupor. Then one day I found "the" book. I started defining the life I wanted. I started making changes in my habits. And I set goals for myself.

And it worked.

I went from having no income in 2008 to:

- Selling my first house in twelve months within thirty days of starting to use these techniques.
- Bringing in $100,000 in gross commission in three months. (January to March 2009)

- Bringing in $300,000 in gross commission the following year. (April 2010)
- Bringing in $500,000 in gross commission the year after that. (April 2011)
- Becoming a Branch Manager the year after that. (November 2012)
- Turning that branch around from #27 to #12 within two years. (December 2014)
- Becoming the Branch Manager for City Branch and turning that branch from #33 to #1 in four years. (May 2017)

So I went from selling nothing for a whole year to selling my first house within thirty days and then selling over $100,000 in gross commission in three months, to being a top performer at Barfoot & Thompson within two years. I went from being in debt and not earning money to being debt free and earning over $100,000 within a year. As a result of making changes in my life, my life changed significantly.

I went from being in massive debt to being the highest performing real estate agent in New Zealand.

This book will tell you in detail how I did that. This is not a memoir, however—it's a how-to book.

If you haven't been able to make a significant or long-lasting change in your life, it may be because you didn't know what was really going on. For many of us, that state of fear and loss is what opens our eyes. But you don't have to go through something traumatic to start enacting change in your life.

You *can* have a blessed life and create incredible change without having to go through intense fear and loss. Part of reinventing yourself is having the right tools and techniques. If you focus your mind, set goals, take action towards achieving them, and contribute to the momentum of your life daily, you'll see meaningful change sooner than you think.

TAKING THE LEAP

After I changed my life, many people have rung me up or emailed me to ask how they can do the same. A lot of them wanted to improve their careers in the real estate industry like I did. This book is for them. But it doesn't matter if you are not in real estate because this book is also for you if you're looking to make lasting change in *any* aspect of your life, professional or personal.

My success in real estate was directly tied to the personal changes I made. One of the biggest changes was learning to select my thoughts each day consistently, a bit like how you select your clothes every day. Living in your head can be the catalyst that creates daily habits that power you forward to where you want to go or creates fears that contribute to a long-term sense of powerlessness. Your life becomes a blame game of whose fault it is that you're not where you'd like to be.

Change is a process. And the process has to start somewhere. Building your momentum will help it accelerate and become easier over time. But to build that momentum, you have to take that first leap.

The leap from inside your head to the real world. The leap from blaming others or your situation to accountability. The leap from your old self to your new self. This is a power you can cultivate.

REINVENTING YOURSELF

The book that changed my life was a paperback published in 1987 called *Mind Power* by John Kehoe. It's funny how a catalyst for your change can come from the most unexpected places.

It was the universe's blend of coincidence and circumstance that led me there. I had been in my state of fear and loss for months by that point. I was depressed, unmotivated. I knew I needed a change. A real one. Call it fate or kismet, but that book came to me at the perfect moment in my life. It was an opportunity to change. And I was open enough to take it.

If you are open to it, this book can do for you what Mr. Kehoe's *Mind Power* did for me.

A focused mind is one of the most powerful sources in the universe. But using a powerful source requires powerful intention. I will provide you with techniques and tools to help you focus your mind towards unlocking your potential. If you think of your mind as a car, I'm teaching you how to drive it properly. Right now, your mind is probably doing donuts on the freeway or stalling out every other mile. But like how a car needs proper maintenance and care, so too does your mind.

To help get you driving your own metaphorical car, I'll bring you along the journey I had to take. It wasn't always pretty or easy. But I know that if you trace my steps from darkness to light, you'll be able to find your own path out to your light too.

I'm not going to tell you how to live your life. Just like how your driving instructor doesn't ride shotgun on every trip you take, telling you where to go. No. I'm going to offer you my own story and tools, things that have worked for me. The actions I took that helped me build success in my professional and personal life. And if that can spark change in your life too, then this book has served its purpose.

So let's get to it.

PART I

The Road to Change

CHAPTER 1

You Have to Take Some Roads Alone

At the end of 2008 after the global financial crisis, I had pretty much hit rock bottom. I was a broke and broken real estate Salesperson.

Why was I broke, you ask? I kept asking myself the same question. It wasn't an issue of effort. I spent days and nights working hard, showing properties to prospective buyers, pitching for great listings. For one reason or another, my deals kept going south. Buyers pulled out. Properties were withdrawn because the market was getting tough.

The worst of it was when a fraudster pulled one over on me. I'd made a sale to this guy and thought things were finally looking up. But it turned out he was placing bids on houses he couldn't come close to affording, all to impress his girlfriend. Just when I thought things were getting better, they got worse. By December 2008, I had a $40,000 overdraft and things were looking pretty dire.

I had been working in real estate for five years at that point. And my performance was average—not the worst but definitely not one of the best. My workplace, Barfoot & Thompson, was the largest real estate firm in New Zealand, and I was working in one of the top branches, Mt Eden, for one of the top managers in the entire business, Ian Gray.

By all accounts, after five years in the business, I should have been a shining star in the sky. Instead, by the end of 2008, I was a pebble on the ground. With high costs of living, my income was really important to help support my family, so it was scary when after a year I was in debt. Being flat-out broke is a humbling experience.

All the more humbling when you have gracious friends who support you. In December 2008, the same month my debt was in the tens of thousands, a good friend of mine invited my family to her parent's beach house in Whangamata, which is on the Coromandel in New Zealand. A week to decompress with my husband and kids and forget about our troubles for a little while. Bless her. Not only was it an amazing gesture on her part, but it led to one of the most significant moments of my life.

One day during our stay, I was wandering around the village shops feeling sorry for myself. Amidst my moping, I found myself in a packed junk shop, full of second-hand items from people's kitchens, closets, bookshelves, you name it. Not a bad way to spend some time.

The shop had several large piles of books, and it caught my eye, so I went hunting for a good deal. Then I came upon a thin book with a large title. I had heard of the book before, but I had never read it. The book was *Mind Power* by John Kehoe. Something about it felt unintimidating, approachable. It only cost fifty cents, which was about all I could afford. Why not? I bought it.

That afternoon I did my first read-through completely on the beach. It took maybe two hours. I am not a speed reader; the book is short. At the end of *Mind Power,* Mr. Kehoe encouraged me to reread carefully. To study all the principles laid out across its chapters and to regularly use those principles. So I reread it. Twice over.

Over the following few days, I read the book three times. After the third time, I made a decision. I would follow the book's principles for ninety days from January to March. It would be my Three Month Experiment. I had nothing to lose. Things could not get worse by trying it out. And I promised myself that if nothing changed by the end of March, I would have to leave the real estate industry (an industry that I love) and find a job that paid the bills more sustainably.

As part of the promise, I decided I would tell no one about my intentions. Not out of fear of judgment or shame. But because it was new to me. I had never done affirmations or visualisations, never tried to consciously harness the power of my mind. These new concepts were difficult for me to grasp. So I knew they might be challenging for others to understand. And I didn't want other people's opinions and preconceptions to distract me from my decision.

Not friends. Not family. Not even my husband. Just me and the universe. I knew that's the only way I'd be able to walk the road to change.

Little did I know then what incredible change was going to

happen over the next three months. Twelve months. Two years. Five years.

THE VIEW FROM ROCK BOTTOM

Think about what you want to change in your life.

Is it your career?

Your body?

Your friendships?

Your attitude?

Ask yourself *why* it hasn't changed yet. I bet you would answer with something like timing, other priorities, lack of support, or just flat-out difficulty. I understand.

What I have learnt over the years of doing this work is that many people won't change until something bad happens or they hit rock bottom. They try over and over, wondering why their effort doesn't bring results. It's because they haven't actually changed their mindset and/or their behaviours consistently every day. Your daily habits are reflected in your daily life.

People learn to become comfortable in their stagnancy. Their routine keeps them aloft. That's why so often we need to crash land to rock bottom. Crash landing is one of the most powerful things that can happen to a person. The sooner you see the bottom, the sooner you can own it, then fix it. Seeing how far you are from your goal often empowers you to allow change to enter your life.

Because people don't fully understand the power of change. But they understand the despair that comes with failure.

I certainly did.

So trust me when I say it's okay to crash land. Society puts a lot of judgment on anyone whose trajectory has any downward movement. We always want up, up, up. Social media has duped us all into thinking everyone but us is on the fast track to success. That we are behind. But a life's path can be a complicated thing. That downward movement is oftentimes what allows us to reach heights we never would have before. It's a turning point. A way for personal growth to enter your life. Failure can be the pathway to success.

And another thing I have learnt—nobody has it all figured out. Even the best of the best. We are all or have all struggled at one time or another. Our job is to push on and be better every day.

STOP THE STORY

We tend to create stories about ourselves. Stories about who we are and what will happen. These stories can cause anxieties. When you tell yourself a story about the future and believe it's going to happen, when you internalise these thoughts, words, and actions, you're directing the power of your mind towards these stories. And so they start to become real. And that is the case whether the story is good or bad.

The power of our mind is a double-edged sword. It can create the change we look for. Or it can perpetuate the failure we expect.

This was true for me. It's part of what led to the downward spiral in my career. When I started to underperform, my mind created a story around my lack of success: *Real estate is a difficult industry. It's hard to make a consistent income. There's only a 15 percent chance of being successful in the real estate industry, so I'm 85 percent likely to fail.*

My mind was attached to this story and ran it on repeat. I was incredibly anxious. So of course, I manifested that anxiety into my reality, and my career continued to stagnate. How could I better myself while I believed I couldn't?

We have to stop the story we tell about ourselves. It keeps us anchored and unchanging. Our minds will manifest what we direct our attention towards, and if we spend months or years believing *We'll gain all the weight back* or *We'll lose all our money if we do this* or *This will end up a disappointment,* it will become the story of our lives. I don't want that for myself. Do you?

You have to reinvent the story. Make a new story. Tell yourself the story of your success. Of your ability to grow and change. Tell yourself the story where you get that dream job, or change that habit, or win that competition. For me, it was to become a top performing real estate agent. You don't have to believe it at first. But over time the story will live in your mind. It will start you on the path you need to be on to get there. Because our stories shape us.

THREE GUIDEPOSTS AND A REMINDER

This might be challenging for you to take in. It was for me. So here are three guideposts to help you as you start to consider these concepts on the road to change:

1. IT'S OKAY TO REACH ROCK BOTTOM

I'm going to emphasise it again because it's so counter to what the entire world tells us. It's okay to fail. It's okay to reach rock bottom. You will never reach a point in your life where you cannot learn and grow from your circumstances. So exercise compassion and understanding for yourself if you are failing. Take a breath. And see about climbing your way back up.

2. TAKE THE RISK

One of the hardest things to do can be to change your habits. People normally hate change. People like to stick to what they know. We like the stories we tell ourselves because it's what we know. And we feel safe in what we know. But real change only comes from being prepared to put yourself out there and take a risk. On the other side of risk is the change you've been looking for.

3. KEEP AN OPEN MIND

Part of what leads so many people to stagnation is a closed mind. We become closed off to truths and concepts that conflict with the stories we tell ourselves. But if we close ourselves off to truth, to our potential, how can we grow? We cannot. Oftentimes, we will end up walking paths we never imagined. Saying and seeing things we couldn't have dreamt of. But that can only happen if we are open to it.

A REMINDER

One of the most powerful things you can do for your self-fulfilment, and your happiness, is to gain clarity on what you want. How do you define success? What do you want in your personal and professional lives? What does it look like?

Too often we define our lives by what we don't want. What we fear, hate, or dislike. But we cannot build the lives we want by directing our attention there. We have to understand the lives we want to build in order to actually build them.

So, to answer the question at the start of this chapter: why was I broke? Because I was lost and because I did not understand how the mind works, I was puttering about with no sense of the life I wanted. I used the power of my mind to perpetuate my failures instead of envisioning my successes. And I needed a wake-up call in the form of a $40,000 overdraft to become open to change. Even if your job, friends, or family are perfectly positioned to support and nurture you, it isn't until you begin nurturing yourself that you will cultivate the success that you want.

So let's dive deeper into the role you play in building the life you want.

CHAPTER 2

Environment Does Not Dictate Success

"You are responsible for your life. And if you're sitting around waiting on somebody to save you, to fix you, to even help you, you are wasting your time, because only you have the power to take responsibility to move your life forward. What matters is now, this moment, and your willingness to see this moment for what it is. Accept it. Forgive the past. Take responsibility and move forward."

—OPRAH WINFREY

Most of us don't know what it means to take responsibility. I certainly didn't when I was growing up. I was a carefree high schooler in 1970s' Auckland with more interest in "tattooing" my friends' fingers during class and mocking the science teacher for his buck teeth than studying or doing homework. The teacher, Mr. Rennie, would try in vain to get the class to pay attention to the curriculum. Instead, we would light up the Bunsen burners just to ignite loose paper for fun.

This was not a good environment. School is a vital setting for our formative years, and my particular school did not have a reputation for churning out high-level academics. It was easy for me to ignore my responsibility and fade into the disinterest of my fellow classmates.

Until it came time for our year-end assessment. Instead of regular exams throughout the year, we had one test at the end. I didn't pay attention all year, so naturally I was not positioned to pass the test. Anything 50 percent or below was a failing score. I was not confident I would get above a 50.

The night before the exam, I realised I wanted to give myself a chance. A chance to pass the test, to be something different, to defy my own perception of myself. So I took the textbook for the class and read the entire thing, front to back, all in one night.

The next day, my classmates perpetuated the story of their apathy. When we started the test, most of my friends sat there, never answering a single question. One girl wrote her name at the top of the paper and left to meet her boyfriend at the beach. Honestly, I was barely much better. My last-ditch effort to study hardly gave me confidence in my answers. But I filled them out anyway.

When we got our exam results a few weeks later, I was shocked to see my score: 51 percent. The lowest possible score to pass. But I did it. I passed. Not only that, I was the only one in the entire class who passed. After ignoring the class curriculum, after ridiculing the teacher all year, after disregarding the textbook until the final night—I still passed.

I changed the story of my apathy and took responsibility, even though it was at the last minute.

That was the first time I realised I had a brain in my head. Not in the biological sense. But in terms of my potential and capacity. Until that point, none of my teachers or classmates encouraged me to take an interest in academics. So I didn't think of myself as smart or clever. But after I finally took my story into my own hands, I understood that no one is coming to rescue you. You are responsible for your life. Positive or negative, your environment—whether it's your school, your job, or your household—does not dictate your life, and you are not defined by your circumstances.

DEFINE SUCCESS FOR YOURSELF

Just as your circumstances do not define you, other people cannot define success for you. Your success is not the same as the person at the desk next to you. If you use other people's definitions of success, you will arrive at a life you don't truly want. It's a simple truth.

Some people are happy earning $100,000 a year in real estate. For me that was not what defined success. I sat down and asked myself: What would make me happy? What really mattered to me? Was it earning $100,000 a year? Was it having a business named after me? Was it having my face on billboards and buses advertising my business?

No. For me, success meant supporting my family while being able to enjoy my time with them. It meant not working twelve hours a day. I could see this life I wanted: I was still dropping off the kids at school, working nine to three, and picking them up at three o'clock without fail. All while earning enough money to give my partner and my kids the lives they deserved. My future felt so clear to me once I finally defined it.

And just so you know, now I am living it.

But creating the life you want is no cakewalk. Defining what success means to you is one of the first steps, and a very crucial one. Once I knew what I wanted, I developed a discipline and structure during my work time that allowed me to cultivate that life. To avoid having to work twelve-hour days, I had to make the most of my six-hour days. Because I knew the goal I was aiming for, it was easy to be 100 percent clear and focused.

Many people want a magical lottery ticket that will give them the life of their dreams. But oftentimes, if they get that life, they feel empty. Examining what you want for yourself is the only way you can start on the path to being successful. On paper, my environment was primed for my success: My friends supported me. My mentor and boss gave me the tools to thrive at our company. And I had a beautiful family of three children with a supportive and loving partner. But I realise now I was not ready to succeed. So I didn't. I had to examine what I was bringing to my situation.

I had coasted through my career for so long, and then suddenly, when things were not going right, I blamed everything around me and never took responsibility for myself. It took a long time for me to see that.

So ask yourself:

What are you doing or not doing that is causing this situation you are in right now?

What does success mean to you? (*Not* what success means to your family, or your friends, or your peers).

SHOVE YOUR EGO ASIDE

So why does it take so long for people to find their own definition of success? To start seeking the lives they truly want?

I think it is because most people hate change or think it is hard.

It's an often-repeated fact of life: people are resistant to change. Many people, in fact, *hate* change. Perhaps it's because if something has to change in your life, you have to admit that you've been doing something wrong. And no one likes to admit they've done anything wrong. No one likes to confront how their choices could have been different, or still can be different.

On top of that, what's familiar is what's comfortable. It's impossible to know what's on the other side of change. So people cling to familiarity, preferring it to the unknowability of change. That works fine for anyone who's happy with their lives. But for anyone who's not happy with their lives, clinging to familiarity leaves you stuck with a life you don't want. I knew that I had to completely reinvent myself to find my path.

I had to find my donkey sanctuary. You're probably thinking: "You're what? Why did you have to find your donkey sanctuary?"

Your calling is your donkey sanctuary. See, there was a highly successful media executive, Ron King, who had a decorated twenty-year career in New York. On paper, his life was "successful" by our society's standards. But he was not happy with his career anymore. He did not want to run the rat race for the rest of his life. However, after stumbling upon a video about donkeys being led to slaughter, he felt he found his calling. He bought a donkey to save it from slaughter. Today, he runs a donkey sanctuary with at least twenty donkeys. You can YouTube him and watch the story online—it's amazing.

Ron King completely reinvented his life. Although people tend to hate change, they only need to find the proper motivation to embrace it. For Mr. King, the motivation was to save donkeys. Perhaps your motivation will find you in some other form.

But you have to be able to shove your ego aside to find that motivation. So many of us start to define ourselves through our circumstances: *I spent ten years studying to be a lawyer, so I'm a lawyer now. All my family grew up to be dentists, so I'm a dentist now. I've always lived in my hometown, so I'm going to stay here.*

This is us latching onto our egos in an act of self-protection. From change, from fear. But even if you followed "the path of the lawyer" or "the path of the dentist," if it's not *your* path, then why are you walking it?

So maybe it's time to stop and *think* for a bit, shove the expectations of others and your ego aside, and find your donkey sanctuary.

TWO GUIDEPOSTS AND A REMINDER

Many of us might be resistant to the idea that we are more than our environment. Or that sometimes the best direction for our lives is away from our previous direction. So here are two guideposts to help you digest these ideas a little easier.

1. YOUR HABITS ARE NOT YOU

It is completely normal for people to have ingrained habits. We are creatures of habit. While these routines and habits may have served us once in the past, we need to re-examine when they are no longer serving us. We are always in control of our habits. Although it can be difficult to let go of them, remember: you are not your habits.

2. YOU ARE RESPONSIBLE FOR YOUR LIFE

No one else is living your life but you. You are responsible for it. Stop waiting for someone to come and change your life for you. Only you can change it. You have the power to create the life you want.

A REMINDER

You do not need to reinvent yourself overnight. A shift in mindset, a change in your belief system, and applying action can happen overnight; however, it can often take time. The most important thing is taking steps towards change.

But first you must get clear on what you want.

CHAPTER 3

Getting Clear on What You Want

"The mind is everything, and my mission is to share my knowledge and experience of that."

—SANDRA FORRESTER

For most of 2008, all I thought about was my debt. The $40,000 overdraft was like a large and dark cloud constantly dangling above my head. The thoughts in my mind were: *Why is this happening to me? I don't want to be broke anymore. I can't be in debt anymore. I don't want to be the company's lowest performer anymore.*

No wonder I was stuck in a rut. I now know that your mind is a powerful tool for manifesting what you direct your mental energies towards. What you put out into the world is what you will attract, and, when I look back, my mind was clouded with doubt and negativity. I was obsessed with the life I didn't want. Since I was putting that out into the world, it was all I would get back. My mentality of negativity spiralled further as I wondered, *why isn't anything changing?* It was because my mind wasn't changing.

But Mr. Kehoe's book *Mind Power* opened my eyes: I *could* change my mind and that could change almost everything in my life. I could have control over everything that I think. I never knew that. I never knew I could take charge of the thinking part of me. Once I came to understand that, I knew I had to start to build an incredibly powerful internal dialogue and belief system. Later in this book, I'll show you how. I am not going to lie, it took hard work, but that system now informs how I behave and what I do every day to bring the vision of my life forward. It has led to my success, a success far beyond what I initially thought was possible.

You may be thinking this doesn't make sense. How can simply changing my thoughts and belief systems change my life? It didn't make sense to me either before I'd been exposed to the techniques. But I put my faith in the process and gave it three months. So, if you think this is just a bunch of woo woo, trust me. I'm a Westie from Auckland, NZ, which if you are in the USA, I guess it's like someone who grew up in Brooklyn, New York, in the 1960s. I was streetwise, but I had no knowledge or understanding about the power of having a strong internal dialogue and belief system until someone showed me how it could ignite the energy around me.

When I made the decision to apply Mr. Kehoe's teachings to my business, I made sure to set a specific goal with a specific timeline. There is power in declaring your deadline and desired outcome. If you focus your intention on those specificities, you are more likely to manifest the outcome with your actions. It becomes more real to you.

Once I made the conscious effort to create a goal for myself, I knew that my largest obstacle was my debt. The $40,000 debt that plagued my thoughts. The $40,000 debt that distracted me from my time with my family. The $40,000 debt that left me anxious and awake at night. I wanted to free myself of that mental burden.

Only then could I start living the life I wanted.

I knew I had to aim high to make a meaningful difference in my life. So I gave myself a three-month deadline to earn $100,000 in gross commission. Even then, half of the gross commission goes back to the company. And after taxes, the half I receive turns out to be roughly $35,000. While it was not $100,000 total for myself, it was ninety percent of my debt. So I was definitely aiming high. Suddenly, I had direction and purpose for the next three months, whereas before I only had doubt and insecurity.

It was the first time in a long time that I felt so clear on what I wanted. And that alone felt good.

ORDER THE MEAL YOU WANT

As mentioned previously, setting a goal is not as easy as you would think. And I was not an exception; I also struggled with setting a goal. I once heard a story about how indecision confuses the universe when it is trying to work with you towards achieving a goal.

Imagine this: you go to a pizzeria with your friends. You call the waiter over and say, "I'll have a pepperoni pizza." The waiter takes your group's orders and heads back to the kitchen. You and your friends chat while you wait.

Then you think to yourself, *wait, what if the pepperoni pizza here isn't good?* So you call the waiter back over and say, "Sorry, I've changed my mind. Can I get a margherita pizza instead of the pepperoni pizza?"

The waiter nods and goes back to the kitchen to change your order. Then you think to yourself, *Hold on, the vegetarian pizza actually sounds delicious.* So you call the waiter back and say, "Actually, can I get the vegetarian pizza instead?"

The waiter looks apologetic and says, "I'm sorry, ma'am, but the chefs are almost done making your margherita pizza."

"Okay, but could I please get the vegetarian pizza instead?"

While you wait for the chefs to change your order for the second time, the waiter comes out with everyone else's orders. You sit there, hungry, and watch all your friends eat. And you wonder to yourself, *Why am I the only one without a meal?*

The waiter is the universe trying to help you get your meal. But you're making it impossible because of your indecision. If you keep flip-flopping with your decision-making, the universe will not be able to bring you what you want. If you don't focus on your desire, the universe cannot help you get it. You'll be sitting at a table full of friends enjoying their own meals while you go hungry.

This is why you have to get clear on what you want. If you don't order the meal you want, you'll spend so much time negotiating with the universe you'll go hungry until you finally realise what meal you want.

YOUR MIND PLAYS TRICKS ON YOU

Your mind's going 150,000 miles per hour almost every single day; it's thinking 150,000 thoughts every single day. You get up in the morning and the same thoughts you had yesterday, the day before yesterday, and the day before that go through your mind again. Then you do the same activities you did on previous days: get dressed, eat breakfast, go to work, etc. Therefore, your brain thinks about the same things 99 percent of the time.

Yet most people don't notice what's going on in their mind.

When I was struggling as a real estate agent, I would wake up every day thinking, "I desperately need to sell a property in order to make money." Then I'd play out scenarios about what would happen if I couldn't earn the money I so desperately needed. The more I thought about those things, the worse I started to feel and the more anxious I became about trying to solve the problem.

To make matters worse, those thoughts and feelings, that attitude of desperation, went with me to work and informed everything I did. Although I tried to hustle business, my desperation continually got in the way of success. Nothing worked because I had the same thoughts and the same belief system about my life. Every. Single. Day.

I thought I had no control over my mind. But I was wrong. You have complete control over your thoughts. You just need to learn the techniques that will enable you to expand the thoughts regarding the things you want to show up in your life and reduce the thoughts about the ones you don't. Once you control those thoughts, you can focus on achieving what you desire.

One of the main laws of physics, the law of attraction, states that your thoughts determine your experiences. It's like gravity; you can't change gravity. So, if you focus on what you want to achieve by changing your thoughts from not having something to having an abundance of it, you will start to see that abundance manifest in your life.

It's one of the reasons that so many athletes become wildly successful. Football or tennis, swimming or basketball, professional athletes have an intense, single-minded focus that drives what they do. They don't get distracted by noise such as partying or vacationing. They're training, dieting, training more, dieting more. They have to be focused and intentional if they want to succeed in their field. It's that intense clarity regarding their desired outcome that allows them to thrive.

I have found over the years that high-performing athletes have similar traits to people who succeed to a high level in business. Athletes are generally very clear on their goal. If it is tennis, it's to win an ATP title or even a Grand Slam. If it's rugby or football, it's to win a World Cup title. If it's Formula 1 racing, it's for a driver to win a podium placing. But in order to get there, those athletes must dedicate their daily activity to skills such as training, mindset, diet, and so on, building their careers from rookies or juniors to levels of high excellence. Success in the business of real estate is exactly the same. There are a set of behaviours and learnt skills that when applied consistently every day will determine how successful you potentially will be. When you combine those skills and set of behaviours with a clear, focused goal, the sky's the limit.

TRUST THE PROCESS

When I first started using these techniques, it bugged me that I didn't understand the process. How does it work? Why does it work? It felt like too much to trust my future to a belief system I couldn't entirely wrap my head around.

I quickly learnt that I had to release my need to understand the process (after two to three years of success, I started to understand why it was working, but I didn't have that understanding at the beginning). Perhaps you think that's ridiculous. But think about it: you do things automatically all the time, without a deep understanding of how it works.

Do you know how your car works? Can you explain everything from how it starts to how the brakes work, why it needs oil in the engine, or why it doesn't just explode for no reason? Probably not. But you still get in your car, put your key in the ignition, and drive to work anyway. You can probably take care of your car better if you understand its ins and outs. But you can drive to work without that knowledge all the same.

The same is true with your mindset. You don't have to understand this process of universal power and energy, or how the law of attraction works. Especially at the beginning of your journey. You just have to do the techniques and it will happen. Just put your key in the ignition, and your car will start.

TRUST THE POWER OF YOUR MIND

With the power of your mindset, just like driving a car, your intention determines your destination. When you utilise your focused mind, energy goes where attention flows.

Focusing my mind helped me define and attain my goals in real estate. When I decided my goal was to write $100,000 in gross commission, I reverse-engineered my path to that goal. If $100,000 in gross commission was my goal, how would I get there? What are all the things I have to do, from the bottom up, to get to that goal?

In New Zealand real estate, the only way to be truly successful is if you have listings and to be always working on a pipeline of vendors (homeowners) who want you to list their properties (you could be a broker or buyer's agent instead, but being a listing agent is the norm). To reach my goal, I needed to demonstrate to vendors that I was the best agent to represent them and their property.

After a few years of selling real estate under my belt, I know that if you want people to believe in you, you first have to believe in yourself. When you interact with a client, there is a transfer of energy between you. The energy you transfer is determined by your preparation for the meeting, your knowledge of the property, your communication style, and most importantly mindset, because like I said earlier: energy goes where attention flows. So, if you are wracked with anxiety and nerves, if you're thinking to yourself, *What if they don't like what I have to say? I'm going to fail this presentation,* then trust me, the client will be able to feel the desperation coming from you.

Clients/vendors want someone strong and confident, with a "success" mindset. Would you say desperation usually inspires confidence? No! You have to get all the negative thoughts out of your mind. You have to *believe* you're going to nail the presentation. And this can't come unfounded either: you need to have done the research and work in preparation for the presentation, which will help you believe in yourself. It's harder to believe in yourself if you know you didn't do the work. But if you put in the time and effort, then you have no reason to not believe.

I always make sure to put the work in so there's no room for me to doubt myself. Before one of my presentations to vendors in 2011, I put 200 percent of my effort into the presentation. I went above and beyond and put in everything a vendor would want to see.

I walked into the meeting and the first thing the vendors said to me was "We've already made our decision to go with somebody else, but we want to see what you think the property is worth."

Most agents would have been mentally thrown and wondered why they were wasting their time being there. Because who wants to spend 45 minutes pitching a presentation they know will be rejected? But I couldn't help but smile to myself. I knew I would blow them away. For the previous two years, I had been unstoppable thanks to the internal dialogue and belief system I had built. No one could do a listing presentation like me. My hit rate was 95 percent of every listing I went for.

That day, I gave one of the most perfect professional presentations I've ever given (I'll explain in full my listing presentation style and skill set in Part II of this book). I finished by looking them in the eyes and saying, "If you believe the person you've already chosen can perform better for you and deliver a better result, then go with them. But if you believe I have got your best interests at heart and that I will do an incredible job for you, then list with me. Don't tell me what you're going to do right now. Just let me know tomorrow." And I packed up my laptop and walked out before they could say a word.

The next day they rang me and told me they were going with me.

IT'S OKAY TO RESET

"For what is worth, it's never too late to be whoever you want to be. I hope you live a life you are proud of. And if you find that you are not, I hope you are brave and have the strength to start over."

—F. SCOTT FITZGERALD

I was able to reach that point after two years of incredible momentum. My successes kept building on each other.

Let's say you got clear on what you wanted, and you started building towards your goal. Then halfway through, you realised: *I don't really want this.*

That's okay. Just reset. If you realise you *thought* you had wanted a particular goal, but don't actually want it, don't keep going towards that goal. Stop and re-evaluate: *okay, what do I actually want?*

Our journeys towards our goals are rarely straightforward. Whether it's an audacious goal of making $100K in gross commission like mine, or something like learning to play guitar, or vacationing in Hawaii.

Take the time to think about what it is you truly want. If you find yourself constantly resetting your goals, it's because you keep returning to your old habits and belief systems. They can be hard to escape, especially once we get stuck in a cycle of resetting.

If that happens, here are some actions you can take to help break out of this cycle (I will also cover this in more detail further on in the book):

- **Create a vision board.** Many people are visually oriented and find it easier to develop towards their goals when they have visual reminders. Try collecting photos or drawings that represent your goals and desires, and place them in an easily visible spot in your space. Pinterest is a great way to create a vision board on a digital platform. You can also print your vision board when it's completed.
- **Find a mentor.** While I hope this book can help you build the life you want, sometimes the most helpful thing is to have someone who can personally guide you on your journey. If you can find a trustworthy person who represents ideas and goals you value, then consider asking if they would mentor you.
- **Take an online course.** There is a wonderfully large collection of growing material online around the very topics I'm writing about here. If you can identify courses that would help in your development, I encourage you to take them.

These are just a few techniques that could help you break the cycle. While you walk your journey, you might find a few tips and tricks for yourself that help you break out of a constant cycle of resetting.

THREE GUIDEPOSTS AND A REMINDER

We've gotten deeper in how you can use your mindset to shape the direction of your life. If you're still wrapping your head around how powerful our minds can be, take a look at these three guideposts:

1. YOUR GOALS DON'T HAVE TO BE MASSIVE

Not everyone has to choose a goal like mine of earning $100K in gross commission. Everyone's journey will look different. All that matters about the goal you choose is that it's what *you* want. Do you want to lose weight? Read fifteen books this year? Quit smoking? Learn a new language? Start a new business? Great. These techniques will help you along your path no matter what your goal might be.

2. TRY NOT TO CHANGE YOUR MIND

Once you get clear on what you want, stay focused. Don't change your mind every day. It's important to reset if you find out your goal isn't what you truly want. But that's why it's important to take time to really become clear on what you want. Otherwise, you'll be the customer at the pizzeria changing your order every five minutes, waiting forever for your meal.

3. CHANGE CAN HAPPEN FAST

It doesn't have to take long to change your internal dialogue and belief systems. If you really put in the work, they can change within a week. What's key is to be optimistic about the changes you're going through. One of my current affirmations is *I'm incredibly optimistic about 2022 and the amazing opportunities that will come my way*. We'll talk more in Chapter 5 about affirmations, but for now just understand that change can come as quickly as you want it.

A REMINDER

If you're still doubtful because this comes across as woo woo, that's fine. Like I said, you don't have to understand how the car works to drive it. If anything, just put your faith in this idea: if you can become clear on what you want, then you can start building the life you want. You can achieve the goals you've dreamt about.

Trust the process, and trust yourself.

CHAPTER 4

Your Mind Responds to the Fuel You Give It

"Nothing I have ever learned or said is more important than knowing that the constant chatter in your head has only the power you choose to give it."

—OPRAH WINFREY

Your mind can be a crazy, horrible, dark place if you let it take you there. But you have the control to get out of the darkness and into the light.

One of the most powerful techniques I have learnt during this entire process is affirmations and visualisation skills. They helped me realise that I was being held hostage by my own concerns, fears, and negative thinking. Affirmations and visualisation skills are undoubtedly the most transformative of anything else I did during my initial Three Month Experiment and then onwards into my transition into one of the top performers in the company. Most of what I learnt about affirmations and visualisations, about rebooting your life and reinventing yourself, seemed so strange at first because I'd never been exposed to the concepts. I thought people can't do that. You can't use the energy of a focused mind, and you can't change your self-talk to create what you want. That's not how it works. You wake up, you live your life, and you go to bed. You don't create it. Wow—how wrong was I.

I'm a very logical person, so the only way I could accept the concept of using a focused mind, of using affirmations and visualisation to change my life, was to put context around it in a way that made sense to me. So I created an analogy where I was a computer and the thoughts I no longer wanted to have were a virus. Self-talk is similar to the software always running in the background of the computer. You are not aware that it's always on, sitting there in your subconscious mind running a negative inner dialogue. Those negative thoughts hijack that software and encode those thoughts as beliefs in your mind. For example, if I say, "I'm terrible at remembering people's names," then I *will* struggle to remember the name of the next person I meet. Why? Because I have a piece of software running in my mind that says, "I am not good at remembering names," which has been programmed from a belief and ended up in my self-talk.

With a computer, you can achieve success by purchasing a new motherboard, replacing the old motherboard, downloading new software, and restarting with a clean system. But I couldn't go to the store and buy a new mind (motherboard); I had to revamp my current thought process system (the software) if I wanted to forge a new pathway.

When a "virus" of negative thoughts came into my mind, repeating over and over again, "What is wrong with me?" "If this doesn't work, I'll have to get a real job to earn money," "People don't want to deal with me," or "Real estate is hard"—I'd stick out my hand like I was trying to stop a car screaming down the street. I'd say to myself, "*No*. Get out. Delete, delete! Those thoughts don't live here anymore." Then I'd think about my affirmations, one of which is that "I am a strong, confident woman. All good things come to me, and I have success" to get my mind back on track.

And it really worked. Over time, positive thoughts and beliefs replaced the negative imprinted ones. If those negative thoughts and beliefs try to sneak back in, I can now deploy my antivirus software, my affirmations, to attack and remove them.

Today, I am confident, powerful, and successful—and whatever direction I choose to go in, no one can stop me.

THE UNIVERSE BRINGS POSITIVE ENERGY BACK TO YOU

I referenced the universe a couple of times now so I should explain to you what I mean by the universe. For me, it means the energy that creates all that is. And I believe that that "energy" is the superconscious mind being creative and responding to your thoughts, words, and actions. There is a lot of talk about the conscious mind and the subconscious mind, but not as much talk about the superconscious mind. If you Google "how do you access the superconscious mind," Google will tell you it is done through meditation, affirmations, visualisation, repetition, music, art, and so on. And, like a magic wand, you can use that superconscious energy to move you towards the things that you want to show up in your life.

It's not always easy to forget past mistakes and failures. A lot of us have had something bad happen to us in the past. For me, it was my failure in my role as a real estate agent and therefore my failure to help to provide for my family. Many people have had far worse than I, and I acknowledge that. But often what happens is we subconsciously decide to let whatever that something was live within us. An example of this is a failed relationship. Many people subconsciously carry the failure of a previous relationship into the next relationship and are surprised when the same thing happens to them again. And so they say, "I am terrible at relationships" or "All men are (insert bad word here)." And, of course, so it is for them.

It was certainly this way for me when it came to my real estate career in 2008. Each time I failed in a presentation for a new listing, I took it really hard. I was an emotional train wreck. But I look back now and realise I was repeating the same mistakes over and over while expecting a different outcome. By the end of 2008, I had made up a pretty strong story about how hard real estate was. Learning about reprogramming thought patterns, attitudes, and beliefs so they're in line with what you want for your life was a revelation, and it sounded easy, but it's a day-to-day effort—you have to work on it every single day.

Changing may sound like a big commitment, but remember, I only committed to my plan for three months. If nothing positively changed, I knew I would have to quit real estate and move on. I knew I had to be intentional about everything from the people I was spending time with, to the material I learnt from. Instead of watching television at night like I normally would, I started watching YouTube videos in alignment with the schools of thought that this whole concept of mindset and *Mind Power* had exposed to me.

I found a whole treasure trove of educational videos. There were YouTubers like Wayne Dyer whose videos reinforced to me that this stuff was real and powerful. Not only that, but there were a lot of people long before me who were practising concepts like the law of attraction and mind power. People like Arnold Schwarzenegger, Muhammed Ali, Henry Ford, even Einstein. So I was in good company! I was just the latest student in a very old school of thought, and I wouldn't be the last either. Each of these people understood that intense focus on your goals, as well as taking actions towards those goals, puts forth a positive energy into the universe that will be sent back to you in the form of your goals being fulfilled.

YOUR GOALS ARE THE DESTINATIONS YOU'RE DRIVING TOWARDS

You do not have to intimately understand how mind power works to use it, like how you do not have to intimately understand how a car works in order to drive. It simply works that way.

YOUR MIND RESPONDS TO THE FUEL YOU GIVE IT

If you cultivate a positive belief system within yourself, you will be able to drive as far as you need to towards your destination. But if you perpetuate a negative belief system within yourself, you might as well be pouring mud into your gas tank.

A POSITIVE BELIEF SYSTEM ISN'T JUST POSITIVE THOUGHTS.

A positive belief system is comprised of:

- **The thoughts you have.** The "software" in your mind that helps shape your energy.
- **The words you speak.** Speaking words aloud gives them power. This is the premise behind affirmations. The words you speak can connect you with others, with yourself, with your goals—or cut you off from all of that.
- **The actions you take.** Positive thoughts and words can only take you so far if you aren't taking actions in alignment with those thoughts and words.

If you create a positive belief system with these three components in mind, you can create a whole new reality for yourself. It's been proven successful, time and again, by folks like the ones I mentioned earlier. Mr. Schwarzenegger, Mr. Ali. I'll be touching more on their stories later. But for now, all you need to understand is this: everything you do attracts something in like energy towards you. So why not commit to a life of intention towards your goals and dreams?

THE LAW OF ATTRACTION

Just like the law of gravity, the law of attraction is a fundamental law of our world. If you let go of a cup you're holding, gravity will bring it to the ground. Similarly, whatever you put out into the world, you will attract it into your life.

We can see this clearly in our day-to-day lives. In every moment, a constant chatter going on in your head. That chatter—your thoughts, inner dialogue, beliefs, everything else going on in your mind—is what fires those circuits in your brain, similar to the circuits that work a computer. Naturally, your behaviour throughout your day is a result of that chatter. As a result, that chatter not only shapes your behaviour but your future. Because our futures are a result of our actions and behaviour.

Your life right now is the sum of your thoughts, feelings, and actions from the past. If you harness your power in the present, you will be able to shape your future. I cannot emphasise enough that you need to align your feelings and actions as well as your thoughts. Some purport the law of attraction relies solely on the power of your mind. But we don't live our lives just thinking thoughts, do we? No, we live with our feelings and actions as well.

This is the foundation of the law of attraction. We will attract what our belief system consists of. That is why creating goals is so powerful. You focus your thoughts, feelings, and actions towards a singular purpose. The more you harness this focus, the stronger your belief system will be.

But how do you begin harnessing this focus? That is where the work comes in. Visualisations and affirmations allow you to articulate to yourself and to the universe what you want to show up in your life. Think of yourself as an actor rehearsing lines for a play. In three months, the show will premiere, but it can only happen if you practise your lines. Visualisations and affirmations operate from the same principle. You repeat these visualisations and affirmations over and over until they have grown into your beliefs and then they start to live in your body. The repetition will prove especially effective if you are able to deliver the words with emotion. When you speak words to yourself with strong emotion, it magnetises whatever you attach those words to, meaning that by putting emotion and repetition into your affirmations and visualisations, you will draw your desired outcome to you faster.

It probably feels like I am saying the same thing over and over again. And you are right. Because over time, repetition downloads these beliefs into your subconscious mind. If you can stay the course, soon your old beliefs and thought patterns will start to change or disappear because your subconscious mind cannot distinguish between reality and what you believe is reality. Creating this new identity empowers you and clears out the old you—the old mindset, the old behaviours, and the old past.

That is the power of the law of attraction.

TWO GUIDEPOSTS AND A REMINDER

The law of attraction can throw people for a loop the first time they hear it. It has always operated in your life, but if you open your mind to it, you can intentionally use it for good.

Here are two guideposts to help keep you moving forward.

1. YOU DON'T GET WHAT YOU WANT IN LIFE...

...you get who you are. The law of attraction dictates we attract what we put out into the universe, and what we put out is reliant on our belief systems. Our belief systems are the sum of our thoughts, feelings, and actions. This can either work incredibly in your favour or keep you stuck in a life of existing patterns and behaviours. It depends on your willingness to grow and change.

2. REPETITION IS THE FOUNDATION OF CHANGE

Let's think of your brain as a computer again. When you want to change your operating system, you install updates. If you want to change, you need to download "updates" to your mind. The most effective way to install these updates is through repetition. You are rewiring your brain from your old belief patterns to your new ones. And once you are able to change your thoughts, your feelings and actions can follow.

A REMINDER

You are constantly creating the life you will live. You create it with your thoughts. Your feelings. Your actions. You have the power to rewrite your stories, change your life, if you are willing to look within yourself and see what you have to change.

But once you look inside of yourself, what do you do from there? If you're ready to hear more about techniques for this process, the next chapter explores the power of affirmation more in depth.

PART II

Techniques

CHAPTER 5

The Power of Affirmation

How do you begin your day? After you wake up, your routine probably looks something like this: make your bed, eat breakfast, shower, brush your teeth, get dressed, and drive to work.

My morning routine was one of the first things I changed after reading *Mind Power.*

Every morning, I would take my dog Taylor for a twenty-minute walk around the mountain while talking aloud to myself the entire time. There was a lot of hand-waving and gesturing involved too. People drove their cars past me and cocked their heads sideways in confusion when they saw me talking out loud to no one (these were the days before earbuds, which everyone now wears, so you never can tell when someone is on the phone talking to someone). Anyway, most of those people who saw me probably thought I was a bit off in the head.

I will be honest and say I was afraid of that judgment, but at that point I had nothing to lose. I was practising my affirmations because I knew they would be foundational to my *Mind Power* experiment for the next three months. And I needed to take Taylor on daily walks anyway. So it felt like the perfect time to practise the techniques and the power of speaking things into existence. I had my affirmations written down in "Reminders in my Phone" so I could remember them and make sure I was saying them right. After a few weeks, I knew them all by heart.

I was really starting to get it: words carry power. Especially when you verbalise them as affirmations. Affirmations are the quickest and easiest tool to enable a change in your mind. Think about it: an affirmation is just a simple statement repeated over and over again. But when you speak affirmations out loud, the physical vibrations from your voice begin the process of quickly affecting your reality and your body. When you commit to the act of verbalising your thoughts, you're actualising them. Giving them a basis in reality, starting in your body. If actualisation can start in your body, it can project and ripple outward into your life.

You've already felt this. There's a meaningful difference between whispering something and saying it confidently, with your shoulders squared. It might seem small. But someone is more likely to hear what you're saying when you project your voice, right? The same principle applies here.

When you *commit*, you are giving intention to your words. When you *emotionalise*, you're helping yourself get to your goal faster. If you say, out loud, "I feel great!" and burst into a smile, you might feel better for a second. But if you practise doing that every day and put your energy in the words and your physicality, your mind starts to accept your intention as truth.

Think of it as general maintenance and care for your mind. You do your morning routine because you want to set yourself up for a good day. You eat, bathe, brush your teeth, engage in physical activity. When you take care of your body, don't you feel better? Why not do the same for your mind? If you want to unlock the power of your mind, you need to take care of it. Affirmations is an exercise to keep your mind in shape.

For me, it was crucial to do these affirmations in nature. There's something about walking and doing things in nature. You're more open and generally feeling more positive. Part of a focused mind is being grounded in your body, and nature helps you with that. While part of me was afraid of judgment from all the people seeing me talk aloud to myself, I also felt more open and grounded being able to practise affirmations with the open air and trees around me.

You can practise your affirmations anywhere you feel comfortable. I've also done them in the shower and while driving to work. Find the place that works best for you, because you can adapt this practice to whatever suits your life best.

PRACTITIONERS OF AFFIRMATIONS

Affirmations have been used by some of the most successful figures in history.

Muhammad Ali wasn't always Muhammad Ali. Before he was the greatest boxer of all time, he was Cassius Clay. Then, amongst other things, he used the power of affirmations to transform himself and attract the life he envisioned. As part of that, he literally renamed and reinvented himself.

Even before he earned his accolades as a world-class champion boxer, he would say, "I am the greatest" and empowered himself as Muhammad Ali. You can easily find it in any of his interviews. He would repeat it over and over again, unafraid to announce it to the world. Two of the most powerful words in the universe are "I am." Whatever you follow it with, those two words are what you attract into your life. His entire belief system—his thoughts, feelings, and actions—drove him towards the destination of "I am the greatest."

And so, of course, he became the greatest boxer in history. Compared to Muhammad Ali announcing himself to the world, my affirmations while walking Taylor seem tame. The bolder and more unafraid you are, the more powerfully the affirmations will work. But you do not need to be as bold as Muhammad Ali for affirmations to work in your life.

Arnold Schwarzenegger is another example of how powerful affirmations can be. He wasn't always the hulking action movie star/politician that we all know today. In his youth, he was a skinny guy living in Austria who wanted a way out of the country after World War II. One day at school, they were shown a documentary about America, and he knew that is where he wanted to be. But he did not know how he was going to get from a rural farming community in Austria to the USA. Then one day when he happened to pick up a bodybuilding magazine, he stumbled onto a vision for his life and decided bodybuilding would be his way out. He set his goal, his vision, and his mind towards becoming Mr. Universe. He set his mind towards that goal and worked harder than anyone else, the same way he eventually set his mind towards becoming a movie star and towards becoming the governor of Los Angeles: by affirming "I'm going to win this.

I am the winner." His incredible track record is owed in no small part to his incredible ability to embed his affirmations into his belief system. His vision became his reality.

THE MECHANICS OF AFFIRMATIONS

Affirmations work more powerfully when they are spoken out loud. That was why Muhammad Ali announcing his greatness to the world was so powerful. So, while you don't have to announce your affirmations to the world, you would benefit much more from physically speaking them aloud rather than just repeating them in your head.

That is because the vibrational energy you generate amplifies the energy around you and more quickly attracts what you are affirming. There is a power in vibrational energy.

Try saying the following aloud—but when you do, *focus* on the buzzing feeling in your throat: "I am aware of the power of my vibrational energy when I speak." Do you feel that?

It's the same vibrational energy as when you hum. Whether you're humming or speaking, there are vibrations that translate from your throat to your mouth and enter the world. Think of your mind as an echo chamber and your mouth as a door to that echo chamber. If you repeat thoughts inside your mind, they will mostly bounce around inside the echo chamber. But if you open your mouth, they will be able to freely travel outside of you and be heard by the world. And once the world can hear you, it can respond in like.

It's really important for you to understand that you don't have to believe your affirmations for them to work. It is better if you do. But at the beginning especially, don't worry about your belief in your affirmations. At the beginning, all you are doing is trying to fill your mind with thoughts that are in alignment with whatever the goal is that you set. Over time, they will begin to embed in your subconscious mind.

In fact, my first affirmation directly related to the subconscious mind. I found this affirmation in *Mind Power,* and it was the first one I spoke aloud every day:

My subconscious mind is my partner in success.

It's important to break it down to understand precisely the idea and energy behind the affirmation.

"My subconscious mind": This acknowledges you *have* a subconscious mind and that you are speaking to it directly. This might sound simple, but think of it like working with a co-worker on a project and never acknowledging them. Perhaps you will both still make progress, but not nearly as effectively as if you worked together.

"is my partner": A partner is someone who works alongside you. A partner works with you. Many people regard their subconscious mind as totally separate from themselves, or even as their enemy. But in reality, your subconscious mind is your greatest collaborator in creating your life.

"in success": This implies that success is already here. You have already successfully attracted to your life who you are. You are continuously doing so. What you need to change is your belief system. But by all accounts, your subconscious mind is performing its functions as designed. So, if you are able to shift your belief system, you will be able to attract a new reality.

This small affirmation of just eight words redefined my relationship with my subconscious mind. It was the first one I spoke aloud every day, and it was the first new belief in my belief system during this Three Month Experiment. Instead of imagining myself as a victim of circumstance, or as someone tossed about by life, I finally recognised my own power.

There is more about the affirmations I used further in Chapter 14, but for now just know that affirmations were the single most important technique I used to recreate myself. They created the shift in my mindset towards becoming the new and better version of me.

THREE GUIDEPOSTS AND A REMINDER

Affirmations will be one of your go-to tools in your "change my life" toolbelt moving forward. But like any other tool, it takes time to learn how to use it effectively. Here are three guideposts to help you as you start to experiment with affirmations.

1. YOUR AFFIRMATIONS MUST BE SPOKEN ALOUD

If you want your affirmations to have a meaningful impact on your belief system, you must speak them aloud. That is the only way to harness their power and release them from the echo chamber of your mind.

2. YOUR AFFIRMATIONS SHOULD BE IN THE PRESENT TENSE

You need to speak your affirmations as if they are already true. The present tense grounds your affirmations more strongly into your belief system. The future is an abstract concept that you cannot really grasp. But you can trick your subconscious by affirming that your affirmations are already true. The words "I am" should always be used at the beginning of an affirmation.

3. YOUR AFFIRMATIONS REQUIRE REPETITION

Repetition is what imprints your new thought processes into your belief system. If you do not employ repetition in your affirmations, you will relapse to your default thought patterns and beliefs. The only way to outgrow your old thought patterns is to wash them out with repetition. This is true with any practice in life: if you only brush your teeth once, the next time you go to your dentist, you will have a mouth full of cavities.

A REMINDER

Incorporating affirmations into your practice is the quickest and easiest way to begin changing your belief systems. It can be as simple as speaking aloud to yourself when you shower, or drive, or walk your dog.

But a vital part of the practice will be getting clear on your goals. That clarity is where your entire affirmations practice will begin. Now let's look at how you can directly apply these techniques within your own life.

CHAPTER 6

Clarity and Consistency

The hardest part at the start of the Three Month Experiment was defining my goal. I made it sound so easy earlier. But my mind was a crowded room, and I couldn't find any space for a goal. I was too overwhelmed by everything going on in my head: *I should add at least five people to my networking database every day. I should make at least ten professional calls per day. I should be pitching to at least three vendors per week.* For the life of me, I could not set my goal after I first read *Mind Power.*

So I read it again. And again. For days after my first read-through, I walked along Whangamata Beach and wracked my brain. My goal eluded me. I thought deciding what I wanted would be the easiest task in the world. Instead, I was stuck staring at a menu, not knowing what to order from the universe.

People get stuck in old patterns of thought. And that is exactly what happened to me. When we first try to break away from our old lives, we encounter our own resistance. It's understandable. But we have to push past that resistance if we want to grow. Otherwise, the fog of our indecision keeps us trapped in stagnancy.

If I didn't make a change, I would be staring at the menu forever, always waiting for a meal that would never come.

I spent days wracking my brain. I wandered down the shoreline those days, lost in thought. Then one day, while taking my walk on the beach, I realised I didn't know where I was. When I looked behind me, sure enough, my footprints in the sand were evidence of my journey to this point. But when I looked around me, I saw a part of the beach I had never been to before. And I had gotten here by taking one step at a time, always forward. I didn't overthink my destination. I didn't stop every few steps to double back and visit a different part of the beach. I just kept moving forward.

Part of the problem was that I thought I needed to completely reinvent myself in one go. But that wasn't true. The truth was I just needed to choose *one* thing. If I could clearly define one goal for myself and put my energy, intentions, and actions towards achieving that one goal, then I would start to attract the life I wanted.

Once I decided to focus on only one thing, it was liberating. I homed in on my goal almost immediately, since it was the topic weighing most heavily on my mind: the $40,000 overdraft. Defining my goal stripped away any feelings of being overwhelmed. Because now my purpose, for the next three months, was clear. I knew the endpoint. Now I just needed to find out how I would get there.

When you define your goal, you should reverse-engineer your path from there. My goal was earning $100,000 in gross commission. So how do I do that? Well, earlier thoughts in my mind—*I should grow my database, I should be networking more*—are actions that naturally folded into my plan of reaching my goal. It goes to show that sometimes we focus too intensely on the smaller details instead of allowing ourselves to dream big.

But the process I'm talking about here is the general structure for problem-solving in any field. Whether it's engineering, sports, cooking, or mathematics, you begin by defining your desired endpoint. In cooking, that's choosing the dish you will make. Reverse-engineering the dish is finding your recipe. From there, you gather your ingredients and follow the instructions in the recipe. So, in actuality, manifesting your dream life can be as straightforward as baking a cake.

You just need to know what cake you're baking.

It was liberating. Because when you have a goal or a vision, everything becomes easy.

THE FISH STUCK IN SHALLOW WATER

On one of my walks along the beach, something in the water fascinated me. There was a fish stuck in the shallow water. It tried to swim forward to push out into the deeper water, back towards the ocean, but the tide always came to push it back into the shallows. The fish flapped its fins with all its might only to end up back where it started.

That was how I felt. That was how anyone who was stuck in a cycle of stagnancy felt. Through all my late nights at the office, all the listings I pitched to vendors, all the properties I showed to potential clients, I was just flapping my fins and ending up nowhere.

If you're not clear on what you want and you try to change, you will expend so much effort only to end up back where you started. Having clarity is the only way to have your efforts take you forward.

But gaining clarity is often the hardest step for most people. Why? Because when you decide to change, you have to accept there is something about you that you don't like. It's hard for many people to accept that. We become attached to our old worldviews to protect ourselves from ourselves. That is how we end up as fish in shallow waters. We don't realise that even as we flap our fins over and over, we have become comfortable in the shallows. The idea of the ocean actually scares us, subconsciously.

If you are able to shed that fear, release your attachments, and embrace your desire, you can leave the shallows. Everyone has baggage. So everyone is in the process of learning how to let go of that baggage.

STRENGTH IN CLARITY

When you decide to do this work, you will be challenged by other people throughout your journey. But when you have clarity, it will establish boundaries within you to protect yourself against these people.

For many years I have been part of a book club—it was a close group of women, and we used the group as an opportunity to stay connected with one another and swap book recommendations.

I'd recently won an award for my work, and I shared the news with my book club group. After four years of using these techniques, my career was at an all-time high. They all applauded and congratulated me.

One of the women in the group asked me, "Sandra, how did you do it? How did you turn your life around? How did you go from being an agent to Branch Manager to award-winning Branch Manager?"

They all seemed eager to hear what I had to say, so I obliged her question. I told them about the techniques, tools, affirmations, visualisations, setting goals, all of it! I was able to change my life with this knowledge. So why would I not share it with anyone who wanted to change their life too?

Many of the women murmured to themselves, curious about this work. Curious if it might be applicable in their lives. There was one woman in the group who was known for being especially clever. Let's call her Diane. Diane was the first to speak up after I shared my story.

She looked at me and said, "That is the biggest load of codswallop I have ever heard. For goodness' sake, who believes in all that sort of nonsense?"

The whole room went silent.

After a few moments, I responded. "Well, I believe it. And the only reason I've been able to achieve what I've done is that I've been clear. I've been consistent. I set goals, I worked towards those goals, and I've proven that it works."

"I just have to say I disagree," Diane said, frowning. "It sounds like you should be on a yoga retreat in India."

I debated whether or not I should keep defending myself. But before I made a decision, someone else in the group piped up.

"Actually, I think what she's been doing is incredible." She looked straight at Diane and spoke without hesitation. "I think we should be congratulating her and supporting her. I don't know anyone who's been able to turn their life around the way she has."

We moved on to other points of conversation, but I felt grateful to both women: Diane, for challenging me, and the other woman, for defending me.

For the other woman, I felt so appreciative that someone had my back. That they spoke up and defended me to someone else who challenged my beliefs.

And I felt appreciative for Diane, who thought everything I was saying was hogwash. It helped me realise no one could change my beliefs without my say-so! Even though she had completely diminished my entire worldview, it didn't have any sort of impact on me. I'd come to a point when I was so clear and grounded in my beliefs and goals that no one could dissuade me.

If you decide to go down this pathway, not everybody is going to feel the same way about the work you're doing. Don't be dissuaded by nonbelievers. Stay focused on what you believe and what you have decided that you want. Apply that to your life. If you are clear, your boundaries around your beliefs will be much stronger and you will find yourself less impressionable to dissenting opinions.

Clarity doesn't just allow you to drive forward to your goal. It allows you to stay rooted in your truth. There is strength in clarity.

POWER IN CONSISTENCY

There is also power in consistency. That is why defining one goal allows you to more potently create your desired future.

A common mistake people make is trying to change ten things in their lives all at once: *I want to lose weight and enter a relationship and get a promotion at work and travel abroad and...*

But if you are focusing on too many things, you're diluting the energy you need to actually achieve one or two things. It starts to become really hard to put all those changes into action. There's a reason you don't brush your teeth a little bit and then go make part of your bed and then start cooking part of a meal and then go back to brushing your teeth, and so on.

On top of the inefficiency of it, it puts too much pressure on you to be able to achieve all of those things in a short period of time. If you put too much on your plate, you won't be able to finish it all. You make it too hard. And you'll feel bad when you didn't achieve all the things you said you wanted to achieve.

Small steps, made over time, can move mountains.

It's important to not to try and do too much. Consistency allows you to actually reach your goals. Focusing on one goal for three months meant I wasn't ever going to be overwhelmed. Being overwhelmed often discourages people to the point of abandoning their goals. But I only needed to change one thing.

I had a friend whose goal was to completely cut sugar of their lives in three months. They started with cutting out chocolate. Then they cut out soda. Slowly but surely, they phased sugar out of their life, and to this day they are sugar-free. They accomplished this over a three-month period. And it wasn't by swearing off all sugar completely on day one. Instead, they took slow, gradual, consistent steps towards cutting sugar out. Dedicating yourself to one goal at a time allows you to meaningfully reprogram your belief system. Consistency in your daily thoughts, words, and actions every single day is what codes those new behaviours and habits into your belief system.

GAINING CLARITY AND EMBRACING CONSISTENCY

Gaining clarity poses a challenge for most people. And embracing consistency often feels laborious. So here's some advice on how to move towards adopting these two values in your life:

Flip your beliefs on their head. Our negative beliefs often put a blindfold on our minds and prevent us from seeing the futures we truly desire for ourselves. I had to flip many of my preconceived notions and beliefs in order to gain clarity. I had to shift away from *Succeeding in real estate is difficult* and *It's hard to make money in real estate,* to *Real estate is the most incredible business for me to be successful* and *It's easy to make money in real estate.* After I flipped those beliefs, I was able to more genuinely define my goal and make progress towards it. It gave me clarity.

Create a vision board. If you're stuck because you can't decide between several goals, create a vision board. Curate a section on the board for each goal you're considering. So, if you're stuck choosing between three goals, create a vision board with three distinct sections. Really put the time and effort to make it visually come to life. Once you're done, take a look at what you've made.

Ask yourself: if there is one thing on this vision board I really want to achieve in three months, what would it be?

Stop and breathe. This process can be overwhelming. Whether you're stuck between several goals or feeling burnt out from adopting a consistent mindset, it can help to stop and breathe. Consider it a soft reset. In your day-to-day life, you are always allowed the chance to give yourself a moment to breathe.

Once you gain clarity, you will finally be able to start walking down the new road you've set for yourself. Imagine your goal as a puzzle you're assembling. If you don't have clarity, you're putting together puzzle pieces without knowing what it should look like. Once you gain clarity, you finally realise what the puzzle should look like once it's completed. And suddenly putting together the puzzle pieces doesn't feel so intimidating anymore.

TWO GUIDEPOSTS

These are the first few steps of your journey. And the skills you gain here will be applicable to every goal you make moving forward. But getting clear and becoming consistent is a challenge for most people. So here are two guideposts and a reminder to help make it less of a challenge than it needs to be.

1. YOUR MIND CREATES YOUR REALITY...

...so be mindful of your thoughts as you start this work. The law of attraction will bring to you what you think about. But if you have clarity, you will be able to focus your thoughts on your desired reality.

2. FOCUS ON ONE THING

You do not need to figure out every part of your life in the span of three months. No one is superhuman. Your life does not need to be completely reinvented in order for you to start enjoying some real change. Let go of the need to wrestle ten different things at once. Stop and breathe. Focus on one goal.

So many of us coast through life. Directionless, purposeless, passionless. I definitely coasted. I procrastinated often too. I had so many things I wanted to do, but somehow, I still found the time to put off my work.

It's because I didn't have clarity. I didn't have a future I was intentionally driving myself towards. If we don't have clarity, we're stumbling through a fog hoping to find *something*. But why hope when you can actually create the life you want?

When you have clarity, you don't procrastinate anymore because you know what you're driving towards. Clarity gives you purpose. It gives you direction. And it will be the foundation of your success.

Once you gain clarity, you will need to actively cultivate your thoughts, words, and actions towards a new belief system. There's a reason we don't live our lives in our mind. As powerful as clarity is, you need your actions to also drive you towards the future you want.

CHAPTER 7

Trilogy of Success

Even after gaining clarity for my Three Month Experiment, I felt daunted by the task ahead of me. $100,000 in gross commission sounded like a lot. I had never given myself such a lofty target before. How was I going to do this?

I reverse-engineered my goal and broke it down into attainable parts. If $100,000 sounded like a lot, then I would just section it off into smaller portions. Since I wanted to make that amount over three months, that meant I had to make $33,000 in gross commission each month.

In New Zealand real estate, as an agent you get commission when you list and when you sell a property. Naturally, you earn more commission when you sell a property you've also listed.

Each listing or sale I completed, my portion of the commission would be $10–11,000 on average. So each month I just had to list or sell three properties. Once I understood that, it felt like a weight was lifted from my shoulders. Just three properties per month? I could do that!

I laid out my battle plan. But now I needed to give myself affirmations that would help me best manifest the life I envisioned. I sat down and wrote a list of affirmations entirely around this goal:

I am a strong, confident woman. All good things come to me, and I have success.

I attract at least two quality listings that result in two unconditional sales per month.

I am an auction expert. I list and sell all my own listings unconditionally by auction.

These affirmations primed me to attract my goal. No "I want" or "I hope" in the affirmations. They had to be "I am," because it would only become real if I already treated it like it was real. Each affirmation was vital.

I am a strong, confident woman. All good things come to me, and I have success. To succeed in real estate, you need to radiate an energy that inspires confidence in vendors, buyers, and sellers alike. If you trust your own ability, other people will feel that and want to trust you.

I attract at least two quality listings that result in two unconditional sales per month. Unconditional sales are when the sale is closed; due diligence is complete, the buyer and seller are moving forward, and there are only a couple of weeks until it moves them in an exchange. No more buyers pulling out, no more sellers getting cold feet.

I am an auction expert. I list and sell all my own listings uncon-

ditionally by auction. Agents stand to gain the full commission if they're able to represent both the buyer and the seller on a particular listing. It was great having other agents bringing buyers to my listed open homes, but for me to reach my target, I needed to try to make sure I sold my own listings. If I did, I would bring in $22,000 in gross commission on average. Just barely shy of my target per month. So this was a really important affirmation.

Now it has to be said that at the beginning of the Three Month Experiment I was not an auction expert and was not listing or selling two unconditional properties per month. But I knew that I had to put out to the universe what my future expectation was in order to attract that into my reality.

So I repeated these affirmations every day. I wrote them down. I spoke them aloud on my walks with Taylor, with my hands waving about. I said them to myself while I waited for potential buyers to meet me at properties. I said it after shaking hands with vendors and closing deals. Throughout the Three Month Experiment, I repeated the affirmations without fail. I took actions towards my goal without fail. Actual reality started to match my inner reality.

Just thirty days into the Three Month Experiment, I made my first sale in fourteen months.

This was a big deal for me. After getting nothing for over a year, I finally sold a property. I remember every part of it: from the buyer calling me, to her picking a property, to showing her around the space, to her making the offer, to negotiating the deal, and then finalising the deal. I knew in my gut the entire time that the deal would go through. After crafting my affirmations, honing my trilogy of success, and taking inspiration from my industry role models, I had a powerful belief in my ability to succeed. And I did.

This was a turning point for me. That sale cemented the power of this work. I knew it was a result of the new skills and beliefs I gathered for the Three Month Experiment. It wasn't a highly lucrative deal, but it was the first positive feedback I'd gotten in the industry in so long. The universe sends you positive signs to encourage you when you're on the right track. And I could feel the universe was on my side.

I knew I had to keep going.

But first, I went home to the kids and told everyone we were celebrating and that we were going to the shop and they could buy whatever expensive ice cream they wanted. Mom had gotten her first sale in over a year.

THOUGHTS, WORDS, ACTIONS

"Watch your thoughts; they become words. Watch your words; they become actions. Watch your actions; they become habits. Watch your habits; they become your character."

—LAO-TZE

I brought my sale in to my boss, Ian, but I didn't say anything about my journey that enabled me to make the sale, because at that point I still wasn't telling anyone about the Three Month Experiment. If I was going to tell him, this is what I would have said: "I followed the law of attraction. I used thoughts, words, and actions, and I am creating a new life for myself."

That's the trilogy of success. Thoughts, words, and actions. I also call it the creative process—not in the artistic sense, but in the sense that you are creating something new in your life that you haven't had before.

No part of the trilogy is more or less important than the other. You need to tap into all three to bring about your new life.

THOUGHTS

Most of us go through our day without taking notice of our thoughts. Our thoughts just float through our head, and we don't pay them any mind. When you live like that, you are riding in a driverless car, moving from place to place. You're just sitting there without contributing to the process of the journey. So how can you end up at a destination you truly want to arrive at?

If you want to change your life, you need to have an active relationship with your thoughts. The first step is simple: start paying attention to your thoughts. It might sound easy. But if you have been on autopilot for most of your life, paying attention to your thoughts can be an uncomfortable experience.

Start by spending a few hours one morning just observing what's going through your mind. What thoughts am I having? What's the purpose of that thought? How often have I had this particular thought?

Most people wake up and have the exact same thoughts as yesterday, and the day before, and the day before. *I have to get to work on time. I hope there's no traffic today. I have to finish this project by the deadline.* If you don't change your belief systems, your thoughts will perpetuate day after day.

But when you focus on a goal, you have to start thinking different thoughts if you want to achieve that goal. If you want to lose weight, if you wake up and think, "I'm going to eat healthy today. I'm not going to eat any chocolate." But as soon as you say I am *not* going to eat chocolate, you're already thinking about chocolate. It doesn't matter that you're telling yourself you won't eat it. It's already in your mind. Your thought processes are the same default behaviours as before.

If you want to lose weight, when you think of chocolate, you should instead think, "Get out. Get out. Delete. Delete. I love fruit and I am looking forward to eating fruit today and will think about fruit instead." And then picture fruit in your mind.

You are retraining your thoughts to think what you want to think. That way, instead of reverting to your default thoughts, you will begin to think new thoughts. Over enough time, and with enough consistency, you will wake up and think, "I should eat some fruit."

Your mind is a powerful thing, and so many of us are disconnected from it instead of embracing its power. If you're going to properly update your mind with new software, you need to consistently retrain your thoughts. It is inevitable that your mind will wander back to old thought patterns, especially at the beginning of this work. But allow yourself to recognise when that happens. Observe what's happening in your mind if you do revert.

I had a big marshmallow problem for a long time. I would eat at least twenty over the course of a day. I knew it was bad for me, but I couldn't seem to kick the habit. My thoughts, my impulses, seemed to elude my grasp each time I tried to retrain them. Then I started practising visualisation exercises.

José Silva created the Silva Method based around visualisation exercises and techniques. The idea was to use mild self-hypnosis to help guide your mind towards your goals. This method is especially powerful for anyone who is a fan of vision boards.

The Silva Method gave me a format to follow in my head to reprogram my mind and kick my marshmallow habit. Here's what it looked like:

- **The thought of eating marshmallows pops into my mind.**
- **I visualise myself eating a marshmallow.**
- **I visualise myself eating twenty marshmallows at once.**
- **I visualise myself drowning in marshmallows, with marshmallows all around me.**
- **I visualise myself with no marshmallows at all. Instead, I have a glass of water.**

Now this may sound simplistic, so I encourage you to Google José Silva on YouTube or you can do the Silva course on Mindvalley.com. Once you understand all the principles, you can adapt the guidelines above with whatever thought you are trying to change.

Although I'm a total affirmations die hard, Mr. Silva's method of visualisation helped me go from eating twenty marshmallows every day to eating none at all. To this day, when I see or think of a marshmallow, I reach for a glass of water instead.

There is power to visualisation, and you can tap into that power to help retrain your thoughts.

WORDS

Be careful with what you say.

Words are powerful vessels of energy. When you open your mouth to speak, you're telling people who you are. Each word you say is a choice: a choice of what energy you're putting out to one other person, to a room full of people, or to even no one but the universe. The power of words isn't restricted just to affirmations. Positive or negative, your words carry weight. And just like a magic wand, what you send to the universe, it will give back to you.

If you feel rooted in your current self-image, you may be unintentionally perpetuating it by speaking it into reality every day. A friend of mine constantly suffers from some physical illness: a sickness, a chronic condition, an allergy. She's quick to say so too: "I've never been a well person. I've always suffered from illness and problems."

Well, if you repeat something over and over throughout your life, it becomes part of your belief system. Since your belief system creates your reality, my friend was actively creating the reality of her own unwellness. Of course, there are a whole host of other medical factors involved, but the fact is that you will only be able to change your situation if you are open to believing and saying the change you desire.

That is why one of my daily affirmations is "I am incredibly healthy, and every day all the cells of my body vibrate with abundant good health and radiant energy." If my friend began repeating this affirmation daily, she would eventually notice some positive changes in her health.

Émile Coué is an astounding example of the power of words and affirmations. Émile was a French psychologist who wrote a book called *Self-Mastery Through Conscious Autosuggestion,* which was published in England in 1920. He is famous for his mantra-like autosuggestion phrase, "Every day, in every way, I am getting better and better." In *The Secret,* there is a story about a man who used this phrase and visualisation after he had a terrible accident where he fell off a horse and broke every bone in his body. Doctors told him he would never walk again. But he practised that daily affirmation: "Every day, in every way, I'm getting better and better." It took a long time, but eventually he was able to walk again.

ACTIONS

I take issue with *The Secret. The Secret* is an incredibly popular book and movie that introduced the law of attraction to mainstream society. However, the movie made it seem like thoughts and words alone were sufficient to attract a new life.

From my experience, that's not true. Your actions, the last part of the trilogy of success, is just as necessary as your thoughts and words. Even if I retrain my mind to think "I'll have a glass of water" instead of thinking about chocolate, if I still take the action of eating chocolate anyway, then nothing will change for me. You have to take actions that are in alignment with your goal.

For my Three Month Experiment, I didn't just practise my

affirmations and sit on my behind. To earn $100,000 in gross commission, I also went to work every day, pitched constantly to vendors, networked with industry peers, scouted new properties, and learnt about how to best improve my practice as a real estate agent.

You can think of your actions as you physically expressing your thoughts and words into the world. If you don't express your thoughts and words through your actions, that disconnect will undermine the power of your thoughts and words. You need to get all three on the same team.

THE HALF-MARATHON EXAMPLE

You don't have to wait until you hit rock bottom like I did to make some real change. All you need to do is synergise your thoughts, words, and actions towards a goal. It can be any kind of goal. Keep it simple and easy. All you need to do is start building momentum so you can give yourself evidence of your own ability to change.

It can be as simple as wanting to run a half-marathon.

THOUGHTS

I want to run a half-marathon.

WORDS	ACTIONS
"I am an athlete who completes a half-marathon."	Buy running gear, like shoes or shorts.
"I am training for my success in the half-marathon."	Research how to train for a half-marathon.
"I am eating well and treating my body well."	Rest properly and eat a healthy diet.
"I am eager to run every day."	Start slowly, but run every day.

The half-marathon example helps illustrate the relationship between the three parts of the trilogy of success well.

The goal begins with finding clarity in your thoughts. You have to be able to decide and commit: *I want to run a half-marathon.* From there, your actions have to be in support of that goal: buying running gear, researching how to train, resting properly and eating healthily. If your actions aren't reflective of your goal, you simply won't be able to fulfil your goal. Having the thought isn't enough. All the while, if you are going to be able to summon the mental fortitude for this commitment, bolstering yourself with your words and affirmations will give you the strength to keep going.

You can use the power of the trilogy of success to do anything from train for a half-marathon, to earning $100,000 in gross commission, to whatever your heart desires.

THREE GUIDEPOSTS AND A REMINDER

The trilogy of success is a wonderful template that anyone can use to facilitate a process of change and growth. Here are three guideposts to help organise your thoughts around the trilogy of success:

1. EVERYTHING STARTS WITH YOUR THOUGHTS

This work begins with you rewiring your brain so that you can download new software into your mind. The first step to your success is a positive mindset and positive self-image. So remember: everything starts with your thoughts.

2. YOUR WORDS MATTER

Be mindful of how you speak to others and how you speak about yourself. What you speak, you speak into existence. Reflect on the messages you've parroted about yourself over the years and how you may have been perpetuating them with your words.

3. YOU CAN'T JUST SIT BACK

For your thoughts and words to have a meaningful impact on your life, you can't sit back on the couch and do nothing. Of course, not every moment of your life has to be spent trying to achieve your goals. But if your thoughts and your words don't match up with your actions, you won't see the change you're seeking.

A REMINDER

You aren't expected to master this process in a quick timespan. This work can happen quickly, but you're allowed to go at your own pace. But now that we've discussed the trilogy of success, you finally have the main tool in your toolbelt for approaching your goals.

Still, starting this journey feels like a daunting task. However, enough knowledge and wisdom from role models, peers, and friends can help lift you forward on your path. Let's see how you can best set yourself up for success without having to struggle by yourself.

As Mahatma Gandhi said, "Happiness is when what you think, what you say, and what you do are in harmony."

CHAPTER 8

Start from Experience, Not Scratch

In February 2009, another book came into my life and left a huge impact. I heard of *Think and Grow Rich* by Napoleon Hill through the bestseller lists and took a look out of curiosity. When I opened the book, I was surprised to see it was originally written in 1937. Why was a book written more than seventy years ago selling so well?

Mr. Hill had interviewed a large group of immensely successful, wealthy individuals and collected their stories into the book. The stories of their successes, the techniques they used, and the challenges they faced.

I had read *Mind Power* three times over and took a leap of faith on its ideas. But with *Think and Grow Rich,* it only took one idea in the book to be a massive game-changer for me. Mr. Hill wrote that, to be successful in an industry, you do not have to reinvent the wheel. Instead, look to who you believe is doing the best in that industry and copy them.

It's a simple idea. But it rocked my world. The successful entrepreneurs, pioneers, and industry giants in Mr. Hill's book all became successful by studying the successes of others and copying them. Why couldn't I do the same?

Suddenly, I didn't have to figure out my pathway myself. I could just study my industry role models and take note of what they were doing and how they became successful. I was in a particularly advantageous position for this. Mt Eden, the branch of Barfoot & Thompson I worked for, was one of the top branches in the entire organisation. And my coworkers were real estate rock stars.

If I could work out the strengths of my peers, I could take my career to the next level. There were four individuals whose skills I focused on. They consistently topped the lists with their earnings, so I identified them as high-performing agents in the field and observed them to discover what I could learn from them.

These four individuals were:

THE MARKETING MASTER	THE LEVERAGING LEGEND
She was an expert at marketing. She had an uncanny ability to perfectly pitch marketing plans to vendors. This was centred around her firm belief in her own ability to market properly to those vendors. She also happened to be a good friend of mine, so I asked to pick her brain repeatedly over cups of coffee.	She was constantly leveraging her networks and communities to drive her stream of clients and sales. Whether it was at the village butcher, at a coffee shop, or at the local school, she would pass out her business cards by the handful. There wasn't anyone in her community who didn't know her name. So, when they needed help buying or selling a property, they thought of her first.
THE DIAMOND UNDER PRESSURE	**THE DATABASE WIZARD**
Her personality was hard to get along with, but she had an amazing belief in her ability to perform in the toughest markets. During the global financial crisis of 2009, she told me that she was happy the market was getting tougher because this would be her time to shine. While most agents underperformed because of the stress, she thrived. What an incredible inner self-belief that was.	Though she started as a personal assistant for an agent at another branch, she quickly flourished into an agent herself and went on to become one of the top performers in the entire company. The reason behind her success was that she had built a thorough database of previous clients, friends, and family, which she used to leverage her business. The vast majority of her business was through repeat clients and referrals.

Each of these women was a prosperous agent in their own right. If I could mimic these four and integrate their beliefs, skills, and techniques into my own practice, I would set myself up for incredible success.

I went into full copy, copy, copy mode. I would attend their auctions and noted how they worked a room. I visited their open homes and listened to them pitch themselves to buyers who could potentially become prospective clients. I even asked a friend of mine to pretend she was going to sell her home so she could get listing presentations from these four, as they each pitched to my friend how they would best sell her home.

Suddenly, I had a clear strategy. I had tangible, real-world evidence from these four women of what builds a successful career in real estate. I learnt things like:

- To be successful in real estate, you need to be a strong listing agent.
- To be more effective, become the lister and seller of the property if you can.
- Prospect consistently every day for at least one hour.
- Sell everything by auction because it has the highest clearance rate of all the different methods of sale.
- Offer high levels of service and you will get repeat and referral business.
- Always go the extra mile with your clients, co-workers, and support team.

One of the hardest parts of the trilogy of success can be successfully implementing action towards your goal. You can have sufficient thoughts and words, and misapply your energy towards counterintuitive actions. By studying the success of those who came before you, you are more likely to set yourself up for success in the future.

THE IMPORTANCE OF STRUCTURE

Studying your industry role models is just the first step. You need to rewire your brain to accommodate these new techniques and tactics. You only have so much time in a day.

If you're going to successfully replace your previous daily habits, you need structure to facilitate that rewiring. Adopting these new strategies won't be automatic; it will take place over time.

If you haven't put any structure into your daily life, the likelihood of you going back to the patterns of the past is very high.

With that in mind, this is the schedule I developed for myself after learning from my four industry role models:

8:00 A.M.–8:15 A.M.	**Drop-off:** I drop off my three kids at their three different schools.
8:30 A.M.	**Arrive at work:** I'm usually the first one in. Clear emails.
8:30 A.M.–9:30 A.M.	**Contact collection:** Identify twenty contacts in my network to call with the goals of having at least ten conversations and setting appointments.
9:30 A.M.–10:00 A.M.	**Coffee break**
10:00 A.M.–11:00 A.M.	**Prospecting:** Call the twenty contacts for brief check-in conversations.
11:00 A.M.–12:00 P.M.	**Preparation:** Organise appointments for later in the day, or collect material from phone calls. Clear emails.
12:00 P.M.–1:00 P.M.	**Lunch break**
1:00 P.M.–3:00 P.M.	**Outside the office:** Show properties, look at properties, or complete appointments with clients.
3:00 P.M.–7:00 P.M.	**Pick up the kids from school:** Kids' afterschool activities, preparing dinner for the family. *No real estate activities whatsoever.*
7:00 P.M.–9:00 P.M.	**Setting up for tomorrow:** Preparation and databasing for the next day's work. Listing presentations in the evening after 7:00 p.m., writing reports.

Consider creating a schedule the same as creating a roadmap for your success. If you lay out the tracks for your actions, you are more likely to imbue each action with intention. Structure is your protective barrier against your past habits.

I was also very intentional in leaving blocks of time in the day devoted to *just* my family. If I didn't establish boundaries, my career would consume my life. And my life wasn't just my career. But I was re-establishing my identity in real estate. That required some rigorous structure.

THE BENEFIT OF EXPERIENCE

I thought I knew how the real estate industry worked. It wasn't until I started observing the best in the business that I realised how wrong I had been in the years leading up to 2009. Their methodologies proved mine inefficient. Their numbers spoke for themselves. I felt like I had been play-acting at being a real estate agent. I was not performing on a professional level. But I finally decided to integrate that professionalism into my practice.

Here is the difference it made: if I put a hunk of wood and knife in front of you and said "Carve a wooden bird," you might be able to hack out something somewhat resembling a bird on your first go. But if you watched an expert woodworker successfully hack out a lifelike owl from that same hunk of wood, suddenly your approach may be very different. You might hold the wood different, handle the knife a certain way, or even carve with a different motion. Your bird will likely be much more birdlike. Whether it's observing the woodworker, picking their brain, or mimicking their technique, you are more likely to have a good-looking wooden bird than if you were to rough it out on your own.

I wasn't the best at working an auction before. Then I made a dedicated effort every Wednesday to attend auctions even when I wasn't participating. I soaked in the atmosphere; I noticed how the vendors and purchasers behaved; I would write copious notes on the entire proceedings; I even used anecdotes from the auctions as talking points in my own listing presentations later on.

At one auction I attended, a property with a starting bid of $800,000 shot up over thirty-five bids to a final price of $1.1 million. A couple weeks later, I told that story to a nervous client with a similar property. And suddenly he was a lot less nervous.

When we gift ourselves the experiences of others, we gift ourselves confidence and authority. It is much easier to trust a method we've seen deliver good results. While I merely adopted their beliefs and practices in the beginning, the more I implemented them, the more they became my own experiences.

My hunk of wood started looking a lot more like a bird.

THE POWER OF WOMEN IN REAL ESTATE

As a real estate agent, you are not just selling a home. Eighty percent of the time, you are also selling a family's future. Their environment, the school zones their kids will live in, the backyard barbecue gatherings, the playdates. You are selling them the rest of their lives.

Now I know this is a generalisation, but, for some reason, women grasp that really well within this business. Women agents understand that when they are working with a husband and wife, they would do well to pay special attention to the wife. Generally, her power over the final decision will outweigh the husband's decision. It's the woman who decides if a house is right or not.

So, whether you are a woman or not, you stand to gain much benefit from examining how women agents conduct themselves within this industry.

You can see this too in how women agents implement structure in their careers. In the real estate industry especially, women tend to be adept at detail-oriented, administrative methodologies. So adhering to an intentional structure is usually no problem for them; that's why so many women in real estate are wildly successful. Barfoot & Thompson is a great example of that. Of the top twenty-five performers at Barfoot & Thompson as of the end of March 2022, fourteen are women—that's 56 percent! That's an impressive figure because, if you looked at the top performers in most sales industries, they would be dominated by men.

When you start to implement a new structure within your professional routine, it requires adaptability and flexibility on your part. Now there are many outstanding men in the real estate industry, but more often than not, women are more willing to orient their schedules around rigorous, intentional structures.

FIVE GUIDEPOSTS AND A REMINDER

Many people believe they have to rough it out to build their success. But while we do have to walk some paths alone, that doesn't mean we have to completely carve out a new path through the wilderness.

So here are some tips and concepts to reinforce the notion that we can learn from other people's successes to help fuel our own.

1. APPROACH SUCCESSFUL PEOPLE IN YOUR INDUSTRY

You would be surprised how often other people want to help lift you up. There's no harm in approaching someone and asking them for a half-hour of their time. If you earnestly express that you want to learn more and improve, oftentimes, you'll get a positive response.

2. IMPLEMENT STRUCTURE INTO YOUR DAY

If you want to build new habits, you need to implement structure into your day. It's your map to success, and it will help keep you from getting lost in the dark woods of procrastination.

3. BE CONSISTENT

The consistency of the daily work is where change is built. While you may learn from others' experiences, you need to personally accrue those experiences as well so they become your truth.

4. STUDY PEOPLE

There is more than one way to learn from other people's successes. You can ask to shadow them and see how they go about their day. How do they apportion their time? How do they prioritise? How do they conduct themselves in certain circumstances? These are all valuable pieces of information. Even if you can't shadow someone, you can attempt to see industry role models in action if you can find public venues where they demonstrate their skills.

5. READ *THINK AND GROW RICH*

And finally, as a very practical guidepost, read *Think and Grow Rich* by Napoleon Hill. If one idea in that book could reinvent my entire career, you're bound to find something valuable in its pages.

A REMINDER

There is power in following someone else's footsteps. Don't be afraid to copy—you can copy, copy, copy and one day realise you are doing your own spin on it. We walk alongside other paths until we can find our own. That's all that life is: learning from others until we've learnt enough about ourselves.

Oftentimes, we need to stretch past our usual comfort zones to find those paths. That can involve practising and rehearsing our intentions until we find what feels right and what is effective. We'll talk more about that in the next chapter.

CHAPTER 9

The Power of Role Play

Sometimes the simplest things can open your eyes to new possibilities.

One day I was at the office, comparing my listing presentation against the listing presentations of my four industry role models. I finally realised my presentation was basic. Compared to theirs, mine did not have enough to wow vendors. I felt silly that I had shown this presentation to vendors for years now.

But now, thanks to my friend, I had a template I could follow and a structure to work from to improve my listing presentations. Of course, I would do my own take on it and put my personality into the presentation.

After working on it over the course of ten days, I put the finishing touches on my new presentation and asked my colleague if I could present it to her and get her feedback. She was eager to help me out. So we went to the conference room, and I performed my presentation over the course of fifteen minutes. When I was done, she just sat there silently.

"So what did you think?" I asked, eager for her feedback. I felt confident. I had done my due diligence and, like Napoleon Hill said, took inspiration from my successful colleagues. This wasn't my basic presentation anymore. It was a kick-ass presentation made by the new Sandra.

"God, it was terrible," she finally said.

I was stunned. It was terrible? I had spent ten days working off the template from some of the highest performers in the industry. How was it terrible?

"Really?" I asked, hoping she might be joking.

"Yes, really," she said. She grimaced. "The content was good. But your delivery—" She shook her head. "—I couldn't keep up with you the entire time. You were speaking too fast, like you wanted to hurry and get to the next point. I couldn't get a single word or question in. I work in the same industry, and I couldn't understand what you were saying."

Apparently, I was delivering information in a machine-gun-fire fashion. It likely overwhelmed or confused prospective clients. Why would you trust an agent who wanted to rush through their presentation like they were in a hurry to get the job done and move on? You wouldn't.

This was some of the most powerful feedback I'd ever gotten in my career. I learnt two very important lessons.

First, I had to slow down my listing presentations and focus on key phrases that made people feel good. If people are going to trust you as an agent, you have to take them on a journey and leave them with the feeling that you are the best choice for the job. Not only do you have to *feel* confident, you have to *come across* as confident. And that means taking time with the material and allowing them to ask questions.

Second, I learnt how vital my energy was in these interactions. When I pitch presentations to someone across the table, they are able to subconsciously feel the vibrational energy I am outputting. That energy determines if they like me, trust me, dislike me, or don't trust me. So I created an affirmation to help give off a positive vibrational energy that inspired confidence in my ability.

A couple weeks later, I role-played the presentation again for the same colleague. But I incorporated the feedback she had given me. By the end, she was beaming.

"Sandra, that was very, very good," she said.

Afterward, just to be safe, I role-played the presentation again with a different colleague. Still, I got very positive feedback.

That is the power of role play.

If I had not role-played my new presentation, who knows how many meetings I would have gone on and machine-gunned my way through the material? It might have taken several meetings of not getting chosen to wonder, "Why am I not getting picked?"

ROLE PLAY IN REAL ESTATE

In essence, a real estate agent's job is setting appointments, prospecting, converting appointments into listings, converting listings into sales, and then repeating the entire process.

With that in mind, mastering scripts and dialogues for your forward-facing interactions is one of the most powerful tools you can hone for your practice. Many agents believe they can wing their presentations and get sales based off of their charisma and intuition alone.

But think of presentations in real estate as final exams. If you don't pay attention in class and just wing the final exam, how likely are you to succeed? Not very likely. Whereas if you "study," or in this case prepare scripts and dialogues, you are setting yourself up for success. Even my one night of last-ditch studying back in high school before my exam meant the difference between me passing and failing. Acquiring knowledge is the first step to success. It allows you to build confidence in yourself to put that knowledge into practice.

Role-playing through scripts and dialogues embeds your key points into your brain so you're prepared for any questions that prospective clients may have. Clients want to see you understand the property. They want to feel like they can come to you for any concerns they may have.

Maybe you think you can distract them by pivoting to other points. But people can feel when you're dodging their questions, or when you don't know the answers. This is why role play is a fundamental basic of real estate that any agent should master. I know that many people don't like it, but then again, many people don't like studying or eating their vegetables! Once you understand it's good for you, perhaps that will increase your motivation for doing it.

If you want to get started role-playing for your practice, here are some tips that will help elevate the experience:

FIND ONE OR TWO PEOPLE YOU TRUST

Whether it's colleagues, family, or friends, find a couple people with whom you can practise these role play sessions. If you already trust them, you are less likely to be self-conscious when you start role-playing. You want to choose people who will give you honest constructive criticism. Ideally, they will already own property. That way, when you pitch your presentation, they will be able to adopt the perspective of "Would I trust this person to sell my home?"

IT'S NOT JUST ABOUT MEMORISING WORDS

If it was just about memorising words, you could accomplish the same effect by yourself with some flashcards. No, part of role-playing sessions is recognising your physical presence as you give presentations. That means your tone, your mannerisms, your energy. You don't want to fill your presentation with long silences and "ums." Also, when you are practising in these sessions, come prepared with your actual visual aids and materials. It will help ground you in the experience and help you understand the tools you will be working with at the actual presentation.

FIND A PLACE WHERE YOU WON'T BE DISRUPTED

Don't practise somewhere you will be disturbed. You will only be able to fully immerse yourself in the role play if you can build momentum through the presentation. Finding a quiet, low-stress environment will help you dive into the role play more wholeheartedly.

BREAK YOUR PRESENTATION DOWN INTO PIECES

You do not have to master your entire presentation in one go. It can be overwhelming to tackle it in its entirety. Embrace the rehearsal aspect of these sessions and break it up into pieces. Start with the easy introductory elements of the presentation. Practise that chunk several times until you've mastered it. Then you will feel much more confident. That confidence will help carry you through the rest of your presentation.

ROLE-PLAYING ISN'T FOR CORRECTING ERRORS

Do not think of role-playing as training bad habits out of you. Yes, you'll want to recognise where you have areas for improvement. But these role-playing sessions are for you to build on habits and patterns that promise the best possible results. It's not a correction of errors.

PREPARING FOR OBJECTIONS

Vendors and clients look out for their own interests. As they should. It's your job to meet their objections with confidence and ease. When vendors have objections, if you haven't prepared, it's likely you'll be caught off guard and lose any leverage you have in an instant. You want to win their trust despite any objections they may have, whether the vendor says other companies offered to cover their marketing costs, or if they're waiting for a certain crisis to end before they make any more moves in the market. That means speaking from a place of confidence in the hope of securing the deal.

HABIT OF REPETITION

In any field, talent alone does not lead to success.

Michael Jordan is a prime example. He is legendary in basketball and renowned as one of the best players of all time. However, he did not coast off of some innate talent. He was known to rewatch gameplay more than any other athlete at the time. In that sense, rewatching sports gameplay is similar to role-playing. You are noticing your habits, techniques, and physical presence. Michael Jordan took the foundation of talent and built it even higher and higher through practice and repetition.

The same could be said for Tiger Woods, Venus and Serena Williams, Michael Phelps, or any top athlete. Any top performer in any field. They are great because they have dedicated themselves to practice.

If real estate was a sport, I would tell you to train and practise on the field. If you show up to a game without training, you're dead weight on the field. Role-playing is real estate's form of training.

THREE GUIDEPOSTS AND A REMINDER

Oftentimes, you will not realise the gaps in your skills until you put them into action. Role-playing gives you the opportunity to recognise those gaps in a low-stakes environment. I'm glad I was able to identify where I needed to grow from my workplace's conference room instead of in the middle of a meeting with a vendor.

When you begin trying out role-playing in your practice, consider these guideposts to keep the process streamlined:

1. ACQUIRE KNOWLEDGE

The first step to success is acquiring knowledge. The only way to take meaningful steps towards that success is if you are able to imbue your actions with intention. Having knowledge gives you an understanding of not only what steps to take next, but a confidence in your own abilities.

2. MASTER SCRIPTS AND DIALOGUES

Winging it won't suffice, whether in real estate or any other field. If you want vendors and clients to trust you, you need to convey to them through your words and your energy why you are the best choice for the job.

3. KEEP IT SIMPLE

When you are role-playing your presentation, break it down into achievable parts. There is no need to throw yourself into the deep end. Make this process as easy as possible so you can move forward confidently. Try breaking your presentation into thirds and master each section before moving on to the next. Then you will be able to put them all together.

A REMINDER

It is very rare that someone will knock it out of the park with no preparation. Even then, can they sustain that success over the long term? If you want to set yourself up for success, role-playing is one of the strongest methods of preparation.

Role-playing prepares you for your part in the real estate ecosystem of vendors, clients, and colleagues. It's important to understand how you will successfully navigate that ecosystem, so in the next chapter, I will be covering best practices for leveraging your relationships in the industry.

CHAPTER 10

Relationships, Databases, and the Culture of Calling

When studying my industry role models, I observed practices that I either hadn't thought to incorporate into my daily routine or took for granted.

One day I was chatting up my colleague Steve. He'd racked up some moderate success at Barfoot & Thompson. But I confided in him and said, "Look, Steve, I just don't have enough listings, and I haven't made any sales."

"Well, when I need listings, I just start calling my previous clients," he responded and casually took a sip of his coffee.

It was such a simple idea. But a powerful one.

Whenever Steve's leads dried up, he would call up previous clients, friends, family, anyone he could think of, and ask if they knew anyone who might be thinking of selling their home. Now, Steve didn't have any kind of robust system to enact these calls. But I recognised the untapped potential I had been ignoring.

So I sought out someone who was regularly databasing to find out how they were doing it. I ended up identifying another colleague of mine, let's call her Barbara, who introduced to me the idea of spending an hour at the top of the day calling up folks to chat and prospect.

She said those morning calls were the foundation of her success.

Barbara emphasised it was key to always have some value to offer in exchange for their time and help. Otherwise, you were just asking others to help you do your job, free of charge. Her solution was to curate a monthly newsletter. It was designed to keep subscribers up to date on the state of the market, but it benefited her by keeping her constantly in the back of subscribers' minds. A month wouldn't go by without them seeing her name again. So, if they ran into anyone who was looking to sell, Barbara would be the first one who came to mind.

Following Barbara's lead, I made my own market newsletter. And each time I ended a call, whether it was with a current client or a prospective one, I asked, "Would you like me to send you a monthly newsletter that lets you know what's happening in the market?" About 90 percent of the time, they would respond, "Yes."

New Zealanders are obsessed with real estate. Everyone is keen to make moves in real estate, whether it's investing, owning their first home, or buying a new home. If you can engage properly with your database, you will find a group of people passionate about the material you are giving them. So, if anything, prospecting in New Zealand might not be as tough a gig as in other countries!

And slowly, but surely, I built a whole database of people who were regularly hearing from me.

PROSPECTING OR THE CULTURE OF CALLING

Prospecting is a word that puts a lot of people off, so I now call it practising the culture of calling. But for the purposes of this part of the book, I will continue to call it prospecting as that is the term that almost everyone uses. It is the most crucial part of the job, and yet it's the part that most agents resist and make excuses around.

In real estate, prospecting refers to the practice of consistently building on your future potential customers. Usually that will consist of connecting with past or potential clients over the phone.

Your power as an agent is derived from your ability to sell, and your ability to sell is based on your ability to connect with people. Hence why prospecting is so vital.

There are three common reasons that agents tend to fear or avoid prospecting:

They believe they have to create a robust database in one go. This isn't true. Successful agents understand that building a database is a step-by-step endeavour. It takes time to develop a network of past clients, friends, and family who agree to receive relevant information from you on a regular basis.

They perceive themselves as an intrusion on someone's day. If you bring forth an energy of "I am an intrusion" to an interaction, the other person is going to pick up on it (even over the phone). How likely are you going to give your time to someone who is already treating themselves as an intrusion? However, if you carry an energy of confidence and convey it through your tone of voice, the speed you speak, and your language, people are more likely to gift you their time.

They had a previous prospecting experience that went poorly. It is inevitable that, as a real estate agent, you will have prospecting calls that go poorly. There are individuals who will take their anger out on you, ridicule you, waste your time, or provoke you. You have to keep moving forward. If you let one poor experience from two years ago prevent you from building your success now, you will stay stuck in mediocrity.

I understood the importance of prospecting, but I was the typical agent, and I did not engage in it regularly. And, even when I did, it was without any real skill set. I knew I had to ramp up my prospecting skills. So I reverse-engineered a prospecting goal that I wanted to reach within two years:

- I wanted 80 percent of my business to come from my database of connections.
- I wanted to list and sell at least one property a week as a result of that prospecting work.

These were lofty goals, but two years felt like plenty of time to achieve them.

Basically, I wanted to develop strong social proof for my clients. Social proof in real estate is the idea that a positive reputation, or reliable actions, will encourage individuals to place trust in you. When they hear your name, you want stakeholders in your communities to think, "She seems to know what she's talking about," or "She might have property information that will interest me."

I needed to up my prospecting game if I wanted to develop strong social proof and meet my two-year goal. And while part of me was afraid, like so many other real estate agents, I knew the only way to progress forward was to *do it.* Of course, I took my time writing affirmations and role-playing to prepare myself for the experiences. Because if you're going to dive headfirst into prospecting, having a solid script for yourself greatly increases your chances of success. Find the words that work for you. Then write them out. In fact, here's what a sample prospecting call might look like for me:

Sandra: *Hi, it's Sandra from Barfoot & Thompson. This is just a quick call; have you got a moment to speak?*

Client: *Hi, Sandra, how are you?*

Sandra: *I'm good, thank you. I just wanted to touch base and let you know that a property that is only fifteen houses away from where you are right now has just come on the market.*

Client: *Oh, yes! I drove past it the other day and saw it had a sign out.*

Sandra: *Yes, that's right. I'm not sure if you're looking to make another purchase, but if you know somebody who might be looking to buy in the area, could you just give me a quick call and I would call them to talk about the property?*

Client: *Yeah, I can do that.*

Sandra: *And would you like me to call you when that property sells and let you know what it sells for?*

Client: *Actually, that would be great because I'd really like to know what it sells for.*

Sandra: *Okay, I'm happy to do that. And if there's any chance I can come and see yours to give you an idea of what it's worth, I would love to do that.*

Client: *Yes, why don't we wait and see what that one sells for and then you can come over and give us an idea of ours.*

Sandra: *Perfect. I will track the sale and give you a call back when it sells.*

It's a very simple get-in, get-out kind of conversation.

The scripts I developed gave me the confidence to plunge into dozens, and eventually hundreds, of prospecting calls over the course of the two years. It became as familiar as brushing my teeth in the morning.

Once I hit my two-year deadline, I was happy to report that I was getting 80 percent of my business from my database. On top of that, I was listing and selling at least one property a week. I had hit both of my goals.

My database was quite hungry for the information I gave them in my monthly newsletters. Not only did they actively engage with my content, but I gained twenty or thirty card-carrying fans. These were individuals who kept my business cards in their wallets so they could pass them around to folks or just leave them around coffee shops. It stoked a lot of confidence in me that I had people who believed in me to that degree.

That isn't to say that the two years towards my goal were easy. No, I had a lot of hard days. Days when my old thoughts and habits would start to creep in. I had to be careful not to lapse back into the mindset that *real estate is difficult* and *I'm not going to land this presentation.*

What helped me get through those hard days was picturing my mind as a garden. The beautiful flowers were the goals and plans I set for myself. Doing and following those goals was watering those flowers. But every day, weeds would pop up. Those weeds would be the old habits and negative thoughts that used to plague my mind. But now that I'd developed a daily practice, I just had to spend time every day pulling the weeds, just like you would in a regular garden.

If I didn't water the flowers (follow through on action), the flowers would die. If I didn't pull the weeds (remove the negative thoughts), my garden would become overrun with weeds. It's a simple idea that can help keep your practice in perspective.

Because who doesn't want a garden full of beautiful flowers?

RELATIONSHIPS AND DATABASING

Databasing and relationship building are everything in real estate. If you do not do them, you will not be able to function long term as a real estate agent.

Adrian Bo, one of the most successful real estate agents in Australia, attributed his success to his databasing skills. He said he wanted to build a client base that would nourish his business for twenty years. His secret? He added literally everyone he crossed paths with into his database and nurtured relationships with them over time. He had reached such prosperous heights of success that he would sell, on average, ten properties a month. That is an absurd number by any real estate standard. And 90 percent of that business came directly from his database.

What was wild was that I did the same thing. In my quest for career elevation, I added everyone who crossed my path into my database. At some point, the connections compound, and, if you're doing right by your connections, they will pass your name and cards along to other people within their lives. You'll have prospective clients call you whom you've never met before. That is the power of databasing and relationship building.

The core of these practices is contact. In our modern age, contact is convenient and widely accessible. Technologies are emerging every day that make communication easier and easier. Back in the day, I would print up to a thousand newsletters to personally package and send off in the mail. Now, I upload contacts into Mailchimp and click "send" to mass deliver my monthly newsletter. But the element of contact is still the same.

You want to slowly build up relationships through regular contact and relevant content. You want to be the first person your connections think of when they decide to sell their home. By keeping in contact and offering them valuable information over time, you establish yourself as a reliable and trustworthy source. Social proof in action.

And there is power in layering your modes of communication to your network. Giving them a call once every six months is the bare minimum of relationship building. But you enhance the results of your effort when you also engage in a monthly newsletter, send "available property" texts, and so on.

Multiple free technologies are available to help empower you to elevate your databasing and relationship building.

Mailchimp: This is a free CRM and mail management service, which remains free up to 2,000 contacts. It's as easy as collecting someone's contact information, populating it into Mailchimp, and just typing and sending the information you want them to receive. You don't have to overthink the content you send out in your monthly newsletter. The content can be as simple as sharing "just listed" and "just sold" sections in your newsletter. Both share valuable information to your network while also establishing your credibility.

Canva: Incredibly user-friendly, this free graphic creation service is an intuitive way to build your social media presence on YouTube, Instagram, Facebook, and other social media sites with compelling and pleasing visuals.

These are just two resources available at your disposal. There is no end to the technologies available that make databasing and relationship building manageable in our day and age. Seek out what works best for you and use it.

THREE GUIDEPOSTS AND A REMINDER

In this chapter, we dove into the finer points of the techniques necessary to thrive in the real estate industry. It took me time to fully appreciate the power of these practices, so here are guideposts to emphasise the importance of this work.

1. DISCIPLINE OF DAILY WORK

Commit to prospecting for at least one hour every day. I promise you that work will add up over time, and in the long term, you will have a well-developed database of reliable contacts.

2. MAINTAIN RELEVANT COMMUNICATION

You do not want to provide information to your network that is completely irrelevant. Know your audience. If most of your database consists of homeowners in the suburbs, why would you inform them about apartments in the city? If you want to add value to their lives, understand what adding that value looks like.

3. START WITH THE END IN MIND

It will be much easier to appreciate your daily efforts when you know what they are building towards. Every day is just one step towards building that powerful database of connections.

A REMINDER

I dove into the nitty-gritty of the real estate industry in these last few chapters. Learning the trade is vital to building a career in this space, but another important piece of the puzzle is getting in touch with yourself and enhancing your ability to achieve change in your life. So in this next chapter, I will touch on what achieving results through these practices can look like.

PART III

Changing Your Life

CHAPTER 11

Momentum Matters

I want to step back in time a bit and tell you a story about what happened just before the end of my Three Month Experiment.

By March 20, 2009, I had not yet hit my goal of $100,000 in gross commission. I was close but not quite there. It was almost the end of the Three Month Experiment. I had ten days to make $23,000 in gross commission. Regardless, I had accomplished an incredible thing. Even approaching $100,000 in just three months was something I had never dreamt of before picking up *Mind Power.* I was still confident I would hit my target, but I didn't know how it was going to happen. I was still doing my affirmations every day, staying positive, and not letting any negative thoughts enter my mind—and I was taking action on prospecting every day.

Then an old friend rang me out of the blue. They'd seen my signboard with the "Sold" sticker on it outside another friend's house. We chatted a bit and caught up. Then they asked me to help them sell their property.

I said yes. It just happened that I had a buyer who was looking for something just like their property. So, after checking back with my friend and doing all the paperwork, I took the buyer to the property for an inspection. It was the perfect property, and they made an offer. I completed the sale. And on March 27, with just three days left in the Three Month Experiment, I hit my goal of $100,000.

Over those three months, I listed three houses, sold five houses, and wrote $105,000 in gross commission. I had not only achieved my goal but had surpassed it.

My boss, Ian, called me into his office. He was astounded.

"Sandra, what happened? How are you doing so well?" he asked me. I couldn't help but smile.

This was the same Ian who, within the past six months, called me into his office because he was worried about my performance. Now I was one of his top performers.

I said, "I've had a mindset change, Ian."

THE PROCESS OF CHANGE

Most people in the modern world want change to come quickly. There is an overwhelming mindset of instant gratification. People walk through life with a "I want it now" mentality that inhibits their ability to work with the process of change. I think this is partly because they see people on social media platforms with what appears to be the perfect life living their dreams. But I have learnt that real change takes time.

In real estate especially, the business is a marathon, not a sprint. You will burn out in the span of a month if you treat real estate like a sprint. The Directors and Branch Managers at Barfoot & Thompson recently identified a goal for the firm: 45 percent market share in Auckland. Instead of attempting a complete overhaul within a month, or even a year, they agreed our strategy would take two years to implement. The firm would take small steps every day to shift from our current standing to our projected endpoint.

On a personal level, the general rule of thumb is that it takes ninety days to change your habits. That is why I gave myself ninety days for the Three Month Experiment. Your mind needs time to reboot and download your new software. Just like how Barfoot & Thompson embraces "small steps every day," you can embrace "small steps every day."

The most common mistake you can make is dropping your goal because you don't achieve it immediately. You aren't going to learn to play piano in one day. You aren't going to be fluent in Spanish in one week. But once you identify an achievable goal, give yourself ninety days and make steps everyday towards achieving it. You will find that is all the time you need to see the change you desire. In fact, for me, it took the pressure off. All I needed was ninety days to gain permanent lifestyle changes. It seemed like a good deal to me!

Those ninety days aren't going to be straightforward for everyone. Many people approach the halfway mark without seeing any meaningful changes. For one reason or another, it happens; road bumps are inevitable.

Do not blame yourself. Forget your past mistakes and failures. You create your reality, and your reality is manifested through your thoughts, attitudes, and beliefs. So be strong and confident about the great things that are coming. Keep faith in yourself. I used this particular affirmation throughout the Three Month Experiment to keep my faith:

I am aware that my vibrational energy attracts all the right people, properties, and circumstances to ensure I achieve all my goals.

If your goal is in real estate, then know that if you are prospecting, perfecting your listing presentation, role-playing with colleagues, practising your affirmations, doing your visualisations, and putting yourself on the right track, that it will happen for you. Hang in there. Keep pulling the weeds in your garden and watering the flowers. By the end of those ninety days, you will see them bloom.

CHANGE HAPPENS AT YOUR PACE

The time it takes to see change varies from person to person. If you are especially open and diligent towards the process, you will see changes happen sooner than ninety days. I was ravenous with the material: after reading *Mind Power* three times, I did a deep dive into other books like Napoleon Hill's *Think and Grow Rich* and watched dozens of videos on YouTube relating to these ideas. I also repeated my affirmations every day and sought out inspiration from my colleagues in the field. I could not be stopped. As a result, I started seeing changes thirty days into the process. My initial curiosity shifted quickly from "This is weird" to "I believe it." The transition in my mindset was a tangible one—instead of the "woe is me" mentality that disempowered me, I took charge of my own life and found power and success I did not have before.

I was living proof that these methods worked.

If you introduced these ideas to a group of one hundred people, ten of those people would actually implement them towards their careers. Can I suggest you be one of those ten? What do you have to lose? You've seen this happen in your own life, or others' lives, before. It is easy for people to go deep down rabbit holes out of curiosity. Whether positive or negative, people have a strong ability to compound their initial curiosities into meaningful parts of their belief systems. The key is consistency and commitment.

If you commit, you will find a strong snowball effect occurs in your favour. After I made that first sale in January of 2009, I had my own snowball effect. Specifically, my energy shift made a wild swing towards the positive. I was on fire! I was given such a meaningful positive response from the universe. How could I now seize the opportunity and keep the momentum going? That positivity and confidence transmitted to the universe, as well as every vendor and client I spoke to in the coming months. They could feel it radiate off of me. Naturally, my successes started to snowball as I approached each deal with more and more confidence.

If you find yourself paralysed by fear at the start, then take a breath and reframe the issue. Small actions at the beginning have the largest impacts later. When I became a Branch Manager, I had a Salesperson, let's call him Timothy, who was the biggest anti-prospecting person you could ever meet. He hated prospecting because he was afraid of bothering someone and interrupting their day.

So I sat Timothy down and said, "Alright, don't worry about calling up twenty folks a day. Don't even worry about calling up ten. You can call two people and consider yourself done with prospecting for the day."

He made his first call that day, and the person didn't answer. On the second call, there was an answer. Timothy was nervous, but he relied on the script I provided for him. He performed wonderfully and had a pleasant five-minute conversation with this person.

He hung up and, with a smile on his face, said, "That wasn't so bad."

The next day he called two people again. The day after, he called three people. After that, he called four. If you fast-forward to today, he understands the importance of a culture of calling, and he relies on his database and prospecting calls for the bulk of his business.

All because he had one five-minute conversation that went well.

Allow yourself to take small steps. Each time you receive a positive response from the universe, take the time to celebrate and download that feeling. As you download more and more positivity into your belief system over the course of the ninety days, I promise you will notice the snowball effect working in your favour.

THREE GUIDEPOSTS AND A REMINDER

Many people stumble before the finish line and allow themselves to stop right before they achieve meaningful change. To encourage you to keep faith and confidence throughout the process, here are three guideposts and a reminder:

1. THE POTENTIAL OF THE FUTURE

There is a powerful quote that helped my mindset shift: "Too many people allow the failures of the past to pollute the potential of the future." Do not self-sabotage yourself by believing in the failures of the past. Set yourself up for success by believing in the potential of the future.

2. KEEP MOVING FORWARD

Don't worry if you are struggling through the ninety days. It is understandable that changing your mindset can be a challenging process. The important thing is that you keep moving forward, despite whatever frustrations or setbacks you may experience.

3. STICK TO THE NINETY DAYS

Give yourself the full ninety days. It takes time for change to manifest in our lives. Even if by day forty-five, or day sixty, or day eighty, you are still not seeing change, then wait. I promise you that if you are consistent and genuine in your process, change will come.

A REMINDER

People begin these journeys dreaming of the positive results they would see. In truth, many people are afraid of the change and reinvention it requires to see those successes. In the next chapter, I will talk about how recreating yourself does not have to be an intimidating process. If you learn to shed your old habits and failures, you will confidently step into your new self.

CHAPTER 12

Recreating Yourself

"I hope you are living a life you are proud of. And if you're not, I hope you have the strength to start over."

—F. SCOTT FITZGERALD

Throughout the Three Month Experiment, I successfully assembled the pieces I needed to complete my goal. Like a puzzle, each piece I added helped the picture of my goal become clearer. I began my affirmations, and the picture became clearer. I took inspiration from my successful peers, and the picture became clearer. The vision of my desired future seemed realer each day.

The final piece of the puzzle was one I did not expect.

As I read Napoleon Hill's *Think and Grow Rich*, he purported the importance of how you look and how people perceive you. So long as you cross paths with other people throughout your life, the impression and impact you leave on them is vital to your success. Now, I'm not advocating for becoming a people-pleaser. But if you are able to emit a strong, confident aura that invites others to trust in you, then you give yourself the opportunity to justify that trust.

Reading Mr. Hill's point on perception, I realised that my impression as a real estate agent was not a strong one. I wore the average "uniform" of a woman in real estate: a "smart casual" attire of dress trousers with a top. If you put me in a line-up with ten other real estate agents, we would all look the same.

To strengthen my impression, I took inspiration once more from my real estate rock star peers. There was a recent transfer agent from another branch who became very successful in a very short amount of time. What did she wear? Outside of work, she wore casual clothing. But whenever she came to work, without fail, she wore a suit: a skirt with a nice shirt and jacket. It was her performance armour. I decided to mimic her.

I shopped around four or five places before settling on an outfit: a skirt with a short-sleeve jacket. I bought two of the exact same outfit so that one could be worn while the other was being dry cleaned. At this point, I had enough faith to try this wholeheartedly without any fear or hesitation. So the next day when I arrived at work in my new get-up, I apologised to the whole office in advance: "Sorry, folks, but you're going to see me wear this same outfit every day for the near future." Some of my coworkers laughed. Most of them were impressed with my new look.

I felt different with the suit on. I *felt* more professional. Part of recreating yourself is being able to see yourself in a new way. Reinventing your wardrobe is an effective and tangible way to accomplish that effect. If you dress yourself for your work, you are literally seeing yourself in a different way. You are also allowing others to see yourself in a different way.

Changing my work wardrobe had an immediate and meaningful

impact on my success. In the entire month prior to my wardrobe change, I sold one property. After changing my clothes, I sold five houses in five weeks. That is a mind-boggling difference.

Clients and vendors took me much more seriously once I wore the suit. They saw me in a more professional manner and felt more comfortable placing trust in me. I looked like a woman who got the job done. So they treated me as such.

I make sure to keep my work and home outfits separate. Putting on the different outfits signals a mental shift for me. When I put on the suit, I am at the top of my game for real estate. When I switch into casual clothes at home, I am leaving work at the door and taking my well-deserved rest.

Either way, the outfit you equip yourself with enables you to tackle the coming tasks much more effectively.

PERCEPTION IS REALITY...

As much as society says to "not judge a book by its cover," humans inevitably make judgments about people based on several factors: What do they say? What do they do? And what do they look like?

People make these judgments to inform their choices. In real estate especially, clients want to find someone they trust with their home. Homes are, 99 percent of the time, the client's most valuable high-ticket asset. Clients aren't going to choose their agent lightly. So how do clients choose their agent? They choose based on an agent's words, actions, and demeanour.

This applies to any industry. Would you trust a lawyer dressed in board shorts and sandals (flip flops)? Would you follow the guidance of a financial advisor dressed like a hippie? In real estate, for me, a suit sends a strong message about how seriously you take your relationship with clients, vendors, and anyone else you come in contact with. Perception is reality. If you allow yourself to come across as strong, reliable, and professional, you simply need to take actions in alignment with those traits to ensure that reality.

True power and effectiveness come when you harness perception and communication in tandem with each other. Because:

- **Even if you are well-dressed,** you can lose confidence by communicating poorly or demonstrating a lack of knowledge.
- **Even if you communicate well and have a wealth of knowledge,** clients may not trust you if their perception and initial impression of you is unfavourable.

By combining scripts and dialogues with a trustworthy demeanour, you increase your charisma tenfold. Charisma is the ability to inspire others to find the confidence in you that you already have. If you hone your communication skills and present a good first impression, you gain the keys to charisma.

...AND ACTIONS SHAPE REALITY

But it isn't as easy as waking up one day and deciding to be different. You need a target you're aiming towards. Perception is reality, but actions shape that reality into truth. Recreating yourself is an endeavour that requires small steps every day.

Reshaping my look was just one of those small steps. It was the *last* piece in my puzzle—not the only one. Each component was as crucial and necessary as the others:

- Researching
- Affirmations
- Visualisations
- Alignment shifts
- Copy, copy, copy
- The trilogy of success
- Prospecting
- Databasing
- Newsletters
- Role-playing
- Attire

Do not let this overwhelm you. I used to feel overwhelmed at this idea.

PICK A PERCEPTION YOU LIKE

When you reverse-engineer goals, start from a destination you actually want to arrive at.

When I picked the real estate rock stars I would model after, I didn't choose people I didn't like. When I picked out suits for myself for the first time, I didn't choose outfits I thought looked horrendous on me. I chose people I wanted to be like. I chose outfits I felt looked good on me. In fact, I took inspiration from characters in *The Good Wife* because I thought their outfits were fantastic. I felt good about myself if my look matched theirs.

If you find yourself resistant to changing your look, then ask yourself: how successful do you want to be in your field? If you want to perform at the highest level in your field, then it is important to wear the appropriate clothing. For me, average success wasn't enough. I wanted to excel. So I eagerly redefined my wardrobe.

Find what works for you and your field. Adjusting my outfit to a smarter, more professional attire made sense for me in real estate. If you want to be a personal trainer, it wouldn't make as much sense. You're more likely to come across confidently if you're wearing reliable athletic wear. It will always come down to copy, copy, copy—what are successful people in your field wearing? If they're wearing legging and tennis shoes because you're a personal trainer, then go for that. If you're a lawyer and see successful lawyers wearing cufflinks, try that. Combining "reverse-engineering" with "copy, copy, copy" will provide you a template for your recreation. It's not on you to create a completely new identity and lifestyle from scratch.

THREE GUIDEPOSTS AND A REMINDER

It's easy to underestimate this last puzzle piece. But it made the difference for me between one sale in five weeks and five sales in five weeks. As part of recreating yourself, you have to develop an exterior that matches your interior.

As you engage with this process, here are three guideposts to help you along the way:

1. MAKE A DECISION

Most people wake up and think the same thoughts, act out the same actions, and go to bed at night wishing they could change something about their life. Make a decision. What do you want your life to be? Start at the end: what does the new you look like? That's always the first step in the road to change.

2. COPY, COPY, COPY

Find others in your field who exude success. Observe how they dress, how they communicate, what they do and copy, copy, copy. Feel at liberty to inject your own style and spin on it. But seek out that template for your success in your prospering peers.

3. IMAGINE YOURSELF AS A LAWYER

When designing your new look, imagine yourself as a top-class lawyer. A prospective client is going to visit you for advice. How will you look when that person walks through the door to meet with you? If you're billing them for five-hundred dollars an hour, how would you need to look to inspire confidence in them? In real estate, you are handling a client's biggest ticket item. You want to inspire their confidence in you.

A REMINDER

Recreating your life can feel like a daunting task. But if you tap into the potential of your mind, you will be able to recreate your life through your own power. In the next chapter, I will be exploring the nature of the mind once more to empower you in trusting in your own potential.

CHAPTER 13

Science of the Mind

"Discovering a new theory is like climbing a mountain and gaining a wider view of the world."

—ALBERT EINSTEIN

About a year after the Three Month Experiment, another book changed my life. Funnily enough, it was by the beach again.

My family and I were renting a beach house in Patua North on the Coromandel in New Zealand. In the house, there was a stack of books for guests to peruse. If you did not finish a book before the end of your stay, you could leave money in a donation box to take the book with you.

I was browsing through the stack when I saw a name I recognised: Napoleon Hill, the same man who wrote *Think and Grow Rich.* The book in this pile, *The Master Key to Riches*, broke down Mr. Hill's insights into twelve principles for success and prosperity.

At this point, I had already been doing this work for about a year. As I read *The Master Key to Riches*, I didn't have the same confusion that compelled me to read *Mind Power* three times over. This time I understood the information. And it provided a deeper clarity for my understanding of the world and this work.

A lightbulb went off in my head. I finally understood: we are living in two worlds.

- **Our day-to-day lives**: when we wake up, go to work, socialise with friends, spend time with our families, etc.
- **Our thoughts, beliefs, and emotions**: the belief systems that constitute our lives and dictate the energy we send out into the universe.

These two worlds are happening simultaneously. And the latter always informs the former:

MY THOUGHTS →	
MY BELIEFS →	MY DAY-TO-DAY
MY EMOTIONS →	

For so long I had disempowered myself. I saw myself as a victim of circumstance. I wondered why life dealt me a bad hand. I only recognised the world of my day-to-day life.

But after undertaking this work, Mr. Hill's book helped it click: I, like everyone else, constantly create my day-to-day. My thoughts, beliefs, and emotions manifest directly into my life. If I believe in the story of my failure, I will inevitably fail. If I emotionalise the story of my fear, I will be anxious. But likewise, if I affirm the story of my success, I will inevitably succeed. If I emotionalise the story of my courage, I will be more courageous.

Mind Power was my introduction to this work. It was like Science of the Mind 101. But after practising the concepts in *Mind Power* for a year, *The Master Key to Riches* offered me the chance to take this work to the next level. It was Advanced Science of the Mind. So I happily contributed to the donation box and took it with me after our stay at the beach house.

APPLYING THE SCIENCE OF THE MIND IN YOUR LIFE

Regardless of your age, relationship status, gender, or career, you can do this work.

Regardless of any failures or successes in your past or present, you can do this work. The science of the mind doesn't belong to any particular kind of person.

If you adhere to the trilogy of success and harness your thoughts, words, and actions towards the science of the mind, you will inevitably see positive results within your life.

THOUGHTS

I am open to the ideas and concepts around the science of the mind.

WORDS	ACTIONS
"I am a strong, confident person."	Reverse-engineering your goals.
"I'm optimistic about the opportunities that will come my way."	Copy, copy, copy.
"I am _____ (complete based on your needs)."	Taking actions in alignment with your goals.

THOUGHTS

Thoughts are the first roadblock that many people stumble on when they first discover this work. If you enter into this work half-heartedly or judge it in the back of your mind—*What is all this woo woo nonsense?*—you will not see results nearly as quickly, if at all. Being open to this work is what allows you to actively harness its capabilities. That is why many people who hit rock bottom take to this work quickly. Like me, they had no other options.

But many people get stuck on needing to understand how the process works before experimenting with it. They are hesitant, or sometimes outright refuse, to try out this new practice before they comprehend it in its entirety. You do not need to understand this process for you to use it. Just like how you do not need to know how a car's engine works to drive to your office. Trust this process. As a baby, when you took your first step, you did not consider the finer mechanisms of your body as you put your foot forward. You just did it. And now you walk constantly without even thinking about it.

Another part of this initial reluctance is that many people are dragging their past around with them. Robin Banks, another practitioner of mind power, explained it this way: while onstage speaking to an audience, he brought out onto the stage a stack of chairs. He used those chairs as an example of how humans drag around our past traumas and use those traumas as reasons for the situation they find themselves in.

He picked up a chair and dragged it behind him. "I was bullied as a child."

He stacked another chair on top and dragged both chairs. "My girlfriend in high school cheated on me."

A third chair was added to the stack, which was becoming quite heavy, yet he pulled those chairs along the stage. "My first marriage ended after only nine months."

He then stopped and said, "This is all of you." Adding more chairs to the stack, he dragged seven or eight chairs at once, unable to take a step forward without expending incredible effort.

That was when I really understood how you can allow what has happened to you to become a weight that drags you down.

Many of us drag chairs from our past behind us. How can you move forward if you do not let those chairs go? If you want to truly change your life, you have to let go of what your life once was. You have to let go of the thoughts that are perpetuating your past mistakes and failures. If you hold on to them, they will continue to define your life moving forward.

WORDS

Affirmations will be your best friend throughout this process. Take time to carefully craft affirmations that verbalise your desired outcomes. If you open yourself to the work and take the proper steps, you will find yourself speaking these affirmations into existence. When you speak affirmations, you are telling the universe what you are manifesting. And the universe always listens. The universe hears you more clearly when you emotionalise your affirmations. Consider this in your day-to-day life as well: aren't you more likely to listen to a speech when it is delivered with passion and emotion?

ACTIONS

When you begin, you must set yourself up for success by keeping it simple. Define your goal. Give yourself, at most, three areas to focus on for one month. Once you've determined your goal, engage with the techniques. Then keep at it, day by day, because consistency is key.

Positive thoughts and strong words must always be accompanied by actions in alignment with those thoughts and words. If you affirm "I am a confident, kind person," then act in an insecure or unkind manner, you are giving the universe mixed signals. But if you employ the techniques I've outlined (e.g., copying, visualising, etc.), you will build the life you envision in your thoughts and words. With your thoughts and words, you are the architect designing the life you desire. With your actions, you are the builder piecing that life together brick by brick.

THREE GUIDEPOSTS AND A REMINDER

Even if you are struggling with these concepts, or still uncertain of your feelings towards them, you can engage with them. Experimenting with them for a month, at its worst, leaves little to no impact on your life. At its best, it can change your life for the better.

As you decide for yourself how you will engage with this process, consider these guideposts:

1. LEAVE YOUR CHAIRS BEHIND

Let go of the past. Focus on the present and look forward to the wonderful future you are creating. If you can let go of the chairs you drag behind you, you will find an ease and openness you haven't felt in a long time.

2. MISSTEPS ARE NORMAL AND MANAGEABLE

It is common for people to default back to old thought patterns and behaviour. When this happens, physically draw a line in the air and say, "Get out. You don't live here anymore" or say, "Delete, delete." Use your affirmations to re-engage your mind with things you want to believe. Defaulting back to your old ways does not mean you are destined to spiral back into your old life. So long as you maintain the consistency of your practices, you will continue to move away from your old life one step at a time.

3. SEEK HELP IN OTHERS

If you struggle to let go of your chairs or manage your missteps, I encourage you to find someone who can help you. It can be anyone who you trust and wants to help you move forward. Though some roads are meant to be walked alone, not all roads have to be.

A REMINDER

If you are sceptical, I was once like you. But if you can find any openness in you, I promise that this work can give you the gift of truly living your life. Rather than being subjected to the motions of your day-to-day, you can empower yourself to define your day-to-day through your thoughts, beliefs, and emotions.

I was able to empower myself to become a top performer in New Zealand real estate. In the next chapter, I will cover my last points on how effective this work can be within real estate.

CHAPTER 14

Becoming a Top Performer in Real Estate

My journey from the Three Month Experiment to today is an incredible example of how powerful this work can be if you enact it in your life.

Let's start with my first sale after beginning this work.

POSITIVE REINFORCEMENT

When I began this work, these were the six affirmations I maintained in my daily practice:

1. I am a strong, confident woman. All good things come to me, and I have success.
2. I am a top performing agent, and I attract at least two quality listings that result in two unconditional sales per month.
3. I am financially abundant and earn at least $30,000 per month in gross income.

4. I am an auction expert, and I list and sell all my own listings unconditionally by auction.
5. I am a top performing agent. I prospect for an hour a day for quality listings that result in unconditional sales.
6. My vibrational energy attracts all the right people, properties, and circumstances to ensure I achieve all my goals.

I spent five to ten minutes every day saying these affirmations out loud. After just thirty days, on January 28, 2009, I made my first sale in fourteen months. I knew this wasn't a coincidence. This was the universe encouraging me after the work and effort I put into my new practice. Using these new skills and beliefs allowed my path to open up to the success I was longing for.

To capitalise on my momentum, I sent a newsletter to my growing database to celebrate my success. I kept the message brief, but instead of an impersonal "I sold a property this month," I wrote out the story of how I met this lovely couple who had been searching for a house for a long time and how I helped them finally land their dream home.

Not long after I sent out the newsletter, I got an unexpected call from an old friend.

"It's so nice to hear from you, Sandra!" she said over the phone. "Congratulations on the sale. Listen, I'm actually looking to sell my property. Could you come over and help us?"

"Of course!" I said, grinning. I had absolute confidence this was even more positive feedback from the universe. *Keep going!* the universe was saying as it sent more and more opportunities my way. If you put in the time, effort, and work, and if you demonstrate your value, the universe will keep sending good things your way.

I upped the ante and listed my friend's property by auction. I still hadn't mastered auctions at that point, but I had a colleague in my office who was generous enough to show me the ropes. As I repeated my fourth affirmation daily—"I am an auction expert... "—I supplemented it by copy, copy, copying my colleague.

At the auction, I successfully sold to a lovely couple who were expecting their first child. It was through marketing that property that I met another couple who asked me for my help finding a home. I ended up selling another agent's listing to them. I felt unstoppable.

COMPLETING THE THREE MONTH EXPERIMENT

Even with all the positive feedback sent my way, as mentioned earlier in the book, I found myself ten days away from the end of the Three Month Experiment and still shy of my $100,000 goal. While many people may have been sweating themselves with anxiety and stress, I knew in my gut that I would reach my goal.

I was barely surprised when an old acquaintance rang me up on March 20 to discuss properties. He'd seen my signboard with the "Sold" sticker outside the house I sold on January 28. Thank you, universe. Thank you, me.

As you know, I sold his property, and, on March 27, with just three days to spare, I blew past my goal and earned a final gross commission of $105,000. In three months, I listed three houses, sold five, and brought in $105,000 in gross commission. That wasn't a fluke, or coincidence, or luck. It was the power of my mind at work.

SETTING A NEW GOAL

Now that I had finally reached my goal, I decided to aim even higher. On April 1, 2009, I set a new goal: I would earn $300,000 in gross commission in twelve months. If I could earn $100,000 in three months, $300,000 in twelve felt ambitious but reasonable (especially because I had decided I would take two months off to spend time with my family).

I adjusted my affirmations to my new goal and spent twenty minutes daily maintaining my affirmations, instead of my usual five to ten minutes. I continued practising my trilogy of success, copying my colleagues, prospecting, all of it.

A year later, on April 1, 2010, I had earned $328,000 in gross commission. Remarkably, I was ranked second in the Mt Eden Branch and had become one of the top performers, which was a big deal because, remember, this branch was full of rock star agents. In the span of one year and three months, I went from the bottom of my branch's performers to very near the top. I also earned a spot in the top hundred performers for all of Barfoot & Thompson. Previously, I was ranked somewhere in the seven to eight hundreds. My growth was astounding.

AIMING FOR THE TOP

I was ecstatic to be the second highest performer in Mt Eden, and people were really starting to take notice of me and ask what I was doing. I was loving this new way of doing business and enjoying the benefits. I decided to keep going and to aim higher once more: I decided my new goal would be to be the highest performer in Mt Eden Branch and earn $500,000 in gross commission.

I observed the highest performer and copy, copy, copied. I learnt a lot from her. I visualised myself being on stage at the annual Barfoot & Thompson convention and receiving the award for being the number one performer. I continued my practice as usual.

By now you should not be surprised to know that the next year, in April 2011, I was onstage at the convention accepting not one but two awards—one of which was for being the number one agent at Mt Eden. Because I had done so well, I had moved from being not just in the top hundred performers for Barfoot & Thompson but to being in the top twenty-five!

Barfoot & Thompson was the biggest real estate company in New Zealand. Mt Eden was the top performing branch in Barfoot & Thompson. And I was the number one performer in Mt Eden. When I accepted those awards on stage, I felt a strong combination of pride and belief in myself. I knew this was my calling. The evidence was the scores of people who wanted me to work for them, the vendors who chose me against other agents, and the company recognising me for my efforts.

It is incredible what can happen in just two years and three months.

WHAT CAN HAPPEN IN JUST TWO YEARS AND THREE MONTHS

I went from being in massive debt to being the highest performing real estate agent in New Zealand.

On top of that, I only worked from 8:30 a.m. to 3:00 p.m. Most other agents performing at this level were putting in ten-plus-hour days. These other agents usually were only able to reach these levels of performance by entering into partnerships with one another or having buyer's agents and personal assistants under them. Meanwhile, I was able to accomplish my success without entering into any partnerships or even working with a personal assistant. I was doing everything myself. I had robust systems and processes for every part of the business and used them to be focused, organised, and efficient in the time I spent on real estate each day.

To celebrate my meteoric success, my husband, Dave, and I took our kids to spend a month in Europe. I pulled my kids from their classes despite their teachers' protests. Sometimes I think schools do not teach the really important things in life, like experiencing the benefits of learning about other cultures, understanding how money works, and the science of reality and the mind (however, I digress). Throughout my entire journey, I've always protected the priority of my family in my life. Life, school, success in real estate—nothing could or would ever take precedence over my family.

The trip was incredible. On my first day back at work after returning to New Zealand, I remember chatting about the trip to a front desk receptionist when I saw an internal communication newsletter on a clipboard and realised something had happened while I was away.

"Oh, the Branch Manager position at the Milford Branch opened and closed while I was away?" I asked.

The receptionist nodded. "I know! Shame that you were gone while it was open."

It was very prestigious to be a Branch Manager at Barfoot & Thompson, and I had applied for five or six Branch Manager positions in the last couple of years. I was always denied. Though the higher-ups did not seem to believe in my potential as a Branch Manager, I still felt disappointed that I did not have the chance to submit my application.

Then another agent, Doug, happened to pass by while we were talking.

"You know, Sandra," he said, piping in, "you would make a great Branch Manager. You should apply."

"The deadline's already passed, Doug."

He shrugged. "You should apply anyway."

So I did. What was the worst that could happen?

I sent an email to the hiring Director, Garth Barfoot, explaining that although I missed the deadline because I was out of the country, I wanted to submit myself for consideration. Garth sent me an email back explaining that Barfoot & Thompson was especially strict when it came to meeting deadlines for job applications...

...but because I was out of the country at the time, they would make a one-time exception for me. So I went to our Head Office for the Milford Branch for an interview two days later.

After that first interview, I decided I really wanted that job. No problem—I had mind power.

I added a new affirmation to my daily affirmations. "I am the new Branch Manager for Barfoot & Thompson Milford by November 2011."

As the process was underway and the new person would be appointed quite quickly, I knew I had to get into "universal action" quickly. So I repeated that affirmation every day about twenty times. I drove to the Milford Branch and cruised past in my car about ten times to get familiar with it and what it looked like. This was because I needed to visualise myself walking in and out the door as Branch Manager. I did my homework and learnt everything about the North Shore, the Milford area, and what the strengths of the branch were. Of course, it was no surprise to me that I was called in for a second interview.

By the time of the second interview, I was ready. I was so well prepared that I was leaving nothing to chance. I even chatted with my Mt Eden Branch Manager, Ian Gray, and asked him for advice about running a branch. It was not in Ian's best interest to potentially lose his #1 top performer, but, to his credit, he supported me 100 percent and helped me hugely to prepare.

The second interview was much tougher than the first, but I had done the preparation work I needed, so I was confident it went well. I continued to do the daily affirmations: I really put emotion into them, and I did a lot of visualisation about getting the phone call confirming my appointment, driving over the Harbour Bridge, and walking into the front door of the branch.

A week after my second interview, I got a call from Peter Thompson, our Managing Director, to congratulate me on being appointed as Branch Manager Milford. I was ready for the call to come—I had visualised it happening.

This was a huge moment for me. I had applied for six other Branch Manager roles in Barfoot & Thompson and had been turned down six times. This was the seventh time, and it was the right time. This process also taught me: never, ever, ever give up. Keep working at your dreams and goals.

I was really sad to be leaving my beloved Mt Eden Branch, my colleagues, and my huge database of clients, but I was very excited about my new career challenge.

NEW STARTS

The Auckland Harbour Bridge cuts the city into two parts: Central/West/South and the North Shore. I operated in Central. Milford was in the North Shore.

The fact that a Central area agent was awarded Branch Manager in a North Shore Branch caused a lot of surprise right across the business, both with other Branch Managers and with agents.

On my first day, I was nervous but excited. The highest performing agent in Milford, whom I had had dealings with before when I was an agent and got on quite well with, surprised me. He angrily let me know that he had applied for Branch Manager and was upset he did not get the position. He then told me he was leaving. He promptly packed up his desk, left the office and never came back. My first day on the job and my highest performer was gone.

I had not expected that. I had my work cut out for me.

The Milford Branch's performance placed it in the middle of the pack of all the Barfoot & Thompson branches, which consisted of approximately sixty branches. Ranked #27 overall, its sales were nowhere near the bottom, but they were also nowhere near the top.

I changed my affirmations again. I had to now focus on where the Milford Branch needed to go to improve performance. One of my new affirmations was:

I am a top performing manager of Milford Branch, who are in the top fifteen of the Barfoot & Thompson network by March 2013.

I had started in the role in January 2012, and I knew I needed time to build the branch's performance. This affirmation was based on my new goal—what I wanted for the future of the branch, which was to improve its current position. So moving from #27 to #15 was a stretch but not unrealistic.

Being a Branch Manager is very different to being a Salesperson/agent. I was now dependent on others' performance and not my own individual performance. So my affirmations transitioned from being about my performance to helping others become top performers.

I instituted all of my winning sales techniques from my Mt Eden sales role at Milford: I taught my agents best practices for growing their databases, which included me personally helping them create a database of previous clients, friends, and family. I wrote their newsletters for them each month and pretty much spoon fed them the process of developing a connection with people. I urged them to embrace prospecting and what the benefits were.

The branch was not listing property by auction, so I put that as a huge focus because I knew how successful I had become by using the process of auction. I ran weekly workshops on Fridays for the agents—it was not compulsory for the top performing agents, but it was compulsory for anyone earning under $100,000 over the past twelve months. The focus was always on income generating activity, such as prospecting, database work, listing presentation techniques, managing vendor expectations, selling marketing plans, etc.

It was challenging work because my performance was now gauged on the performance of others. But I soon got into the swing of it, and I knew things were tracking in the right direction because the branch was listing more property and selling more property than in the previous year.

Just like when I was looking to become a top performing agent, I looked to who were the top performing Branch Managers within the business. I was a pest when it came to asking for advice and help from others. When writing this book, I looked back on previous emails I had sent to other managers when I had questions or needed help on issues, and I was probably quite annoying to some, but I knew that in order to learn fast, I had to tap into the knowledge and experience of others.

After the first year, Milford Branch went from #27 to #18.

Things were definitely tracking in the right direction.

After two years, Milford had jumped again from #18 to #12 overall. My team was incredible. They took to my management style, they adopted the best practise techniques, and most of them really started driving their business forward. They were a dream team.

After about two years of working at Milford, one day while I was driving around visiting new listings, I had a call from one of the Senior Management Team at our Head Office. He said a long-standing Branch Manager was retiring after thirty-plus years with the company and asked if I had thought about applying. I said no because it was a much lower-performing branch than Milford, plus applications had closed already for the job (yes, again). He encouraged me to apply.

I really had to think about this. The branch was City Branch. Based right in the heart of the CBD of Auckland, it had a focus on the apartment market, off plan projects, and credit recovery work with banks and finance companies. I had no idea about any of this business; in fact, it sounded downright scary. Plus, and most importantly, City Branch ranked #33 overall at Barfoot & Thompson. I said I would have to think about it and asked if I could come back to him. That weekend I did a lot of research. I investigated the apartment market, how project selling worked, what the status of the CBD was with regard to growth and property values and what the volumes of business were when looking at all the figures. I also looked at the property management size of City Branch. Nearly all Barfoot & Thompson branches run portfolios of property they manage on behalf of landlords, and City Branch had one of the biggest portfolios in the company.

I could not see any of the actual figures for the branch because you can only look at the profit and loss accounts if you apply for the job, so I had to make assumptions based on what I knew about Milford Branch.

After thinking it through, I decided to apply for the position. I was definitely curious and wanted to know more.

Once again, I told nobody what I was doing.

The first interview was more about me asking the Directors questions. I needed to know what the true nature of the branch was, where the strengths and weaknesses were, and what the Directors' expectations were of the new Branch Manager. By this time, the Directors already knew who I was and, I guess, what I was capable of because I had taken Milford Branch from #27 to #12 in just two years.

I got a call a few days later to ask if I would come in for a second interview. Now things were getting serious. I was either going to be all in or withdraw my application and stay put at Milford Branch.

There is one thing I know about myself and that is I love a challenge. I decided to go all in.

Once I had made that decision, I began the process of using my skills from *Mind Power* and changed my affirmations and visualisations. I began the same process that I had for Milford Branch. I drove past the branch, I saw myself walking in the door as Branch Manager, I visualised the phone call coming to say I had been appointed.

My second interview went really well. I was confident and I knew what had to be done to turn that branch around.

A few days later, I got the phone call from Peter Thompson, the Managing Director of Barfoot & Thompson, to congratulate me.

I had gotten the job. It was December 2013, almost exactly two years since I had been appointed to Milford Branch.

I was very happy but also sad; it meant I would be leaving the incredible team at Milford Branch who were all incredibly wonderful people.

What happened next was surprising. I had phone calls coming in from other Branch Managers all across the company. They were confused and asked things like:

"What are you doing, Sandra?! Branch Managers usually go upward for their next position, to bigger or better achieving branches."

And

"What are you doing, Sandra?! City Branch is a big step back from Milford."

To be honest, I understood their questioning my decision, but I felt like City Branch was the next step for me. By that point, I'd learnt to trust my gut feelings, to go where the universe was encouraging me to go.

Moving to City Branch was a huge shock. The first day I walked in the door of the branch was to meet the outgoing Manager for a handover. I had never been to the branch before that day. I remember thinking, *My goodness, this place is huge.* During the handover chat, the outgoing Branch Manager told me that I should not come in here and try to change anything and to leave the agents alone—they did not need me meddling in their business.

Although I didn't tell him, that was never going to work for me. I am the polar opposite to leaving people alone. My style is to be all over everything, what's happening, what deals are on the go, who needs training, what support is required, and so on.

And that is exactly what I did at City Branch. It took me a few months to get my feet because the City Branch model was so different to almost every other branch in the Barfoot & Thompson network, but by the new financial year, which started April 1, 2014, I was on track.

With the help of the existing Sales Manager, Els de Jong, we shook that place up. I hired a new Property Manager, Tracey Boyle, who was one of the best in the industry.

Three women took that place by storm over the next year, and by May 2015, the branch had gone from #33 when I took over fifteen months prior to #6 in 2015. That is a monumental turnaround even if I must say so myself.

But that was only the beginning.

A year later, we were once again being awarded; this time we got to #5.

Of course, you know what happened next. It was time to reset and shift it up again.

With Tracey and Els on board, we set the goal to be #1.

This was never going to be easy. Remember, Barfoot & Thompson is the largest agency in Auckland, and Auckland is the biggest market in New Zealand for real estate. The type of volume business we needed to do was massive but was definitely achievable.

I could go into lots of details of how things played out that year, but I will not. I will, however, tell you one story about the lead up to the big awards evening.

My niece who lived in Australia was getting married, and her wedding was planned for the weekend before the Barfoot & Thompson awards evening. The whole family were making the trip to Rockhampton (in Queensland) and afterwards going on a holiday together for a week.

That meant I would not be flying back into NZ until the day after the awards.

The whole awards process is very confidential, so we do not know who has won what until the night. So there was no way I was missing that awards ceremony! My husband, my kids, and the rest of the family were all booked to fly out on the Saturday afternoon, but I changed my ticket, left them all there, and flew back on Thursday night.

Awards day came and went in a blur. City Branch won so many awards I lost count.

Our agents won multiple awards.

Our property management won the #1 award for best PM in the company.

One of my rookie agents won Rookie of the Year.

And to top it all off, we won #1 Branch of the Year.

City Branch ranked first overall out of all the branches at Barfoot & Thompson. City Branch went from #33 to being one of the top ten branches and then the #1 branch in just four years.

This was a giant-sized team effort. We all did the work and turned around City Branch. It had happened the same way I turned around Milford: getting close with the agents, teaching best practices, and encouraging them to embrace their power.

However, I do not tell you this story to impress you—but to impress upon you the significance of what this mind transformational work was having on me.

YOUR NEW START

What I've done, you are also capable of accomplishing.

If the numbers and accolades intimidate you, reduce my journey down to its core: I was a woman who was almost at the stage of giving up.

I had a serious case of give-up-itis.

However, I bought a book for fifty cents, learnt a whole lot of new techniques and skills, set a goal, was consistent everyday with the set of behaviours I needed to be successful, and met that goal within three months. And then I did that over and over again. If the speed of my success intimidates you, consider: I was a broke and mediocre agent for many years before my breakthrough.

You do not have to become an ace pilot, or best-selling novelist, or celebrity chef, or famous lawyer, or renowned banker over the span of a month. If you become clear on your desires set achievable goals, and make slow, progressive change, then you can do what I did.

Setting goals: Most people don't set goals. People play around with goals and toy with the ideas of them in their mind. But truly setting a goal means becoming clear and asserting your intention. There was a study conducted by Harvard that found that in a class of graduating students, in the lead up to them leaving college, 84 percent of the class had set no goals at all; 13 percent had set written goals but had no concrete plans; and 3 percent had written goals and had concrete plans. Ten years later, researchers went back and studied that cohort and found that the 3 percent of the class that had written goals and concrete plans were earning ten times as much as the other 97 percent of the class.

Slow, progressive change: Your success is dependent on the work and effort you put in every day. You can see this in real estate: your success depends on the daily work you do. Are you prospecting? Are you building your database? Are you finding properties? Even if you are not in real estate, consider the daily work that is necessary to succeed in your field.

And remember that the work you do today will show you its benefits tomorrow.

The work you do tomorrow will show you its benefits next week.

The work you do next week will show you its benefits next month.

If you make slow, progressive change towards the goals you've set, you will reach your destination. Do not allow yourself to get distracted. Keep your focus. Very often people will be challenged in their day-to-day by other stuff that demands their time, energy, and attention. But if you keep a laser-focus on your priorities, you can keep moving forward.

THREE GUIDEPOSTS AND A REMINDER

My journey from that beach where I first read *Mind Power* to today has been a mind-boggling one. But through it all, I've maintained a confidence and focus that has brought me a life I thought I would only ever dream about.

As you come near the end of this book, I would like to share three more guideposts to assist you at the start of your journey:

1. BELIEVE AND DO AFFIRMATIONS & VISUALISATIONS EVERY DAY

Affirmations and visualisations are the bread and butter of this work. You are speaking and seeing your desired life into existence. If you can say it and see it, you are on the road to the life you want.

2. DON'T USE NEGATIVE AFFIRMATIONS

Do not employ affirmations that operate in the negative. Statements like "I am so broke" or "I am so tired all the time" only reinforce those negative ideas throughout your life. Focus on the positive and affirm the qualities and traits you actively desire.

3. DO THE DAILY WORK

Take the daily steps to practise this work. I only spent five to ten minutes daily completing affirmations at the start of my journey. If you can commit at least that much time, you will make a meaningful difference in your life.

A REMINDER

Wherever you are in your life, you are never too far gone from the life you dream about. I thought I was. But here I am now, writing to you about my wonderful journey from being a middle-of-the-pack agent to having run the top branch in all of New Zealand.

If it's possible for me, it's possible for you.

Conclusion

"When we are no longer able to change our situation, we are challenged to change ourselves."

—SHERYL SANDBERG

The mind is everything.

If you take nothing else out of this book, the most important message I would like you to understand is that your internal self-talk or inner dialogue dictates your external life. The thoughts that you think, the words that you speak, and the emotions you express are what manifests in your day-to-day life.

When bad things occur in our day-to-day lives—heartbreak, financial instability, career missteps—it is often because there is something we must address in our internal lives. A mentality, a fear, an anxiety, a negative self-story, something that perpetuates negativity. That "bad thing" is an opportunity for course correction.

Oprah Winfrey was once sued by the Texas cattle industry after she said on her television show that she never wanted to eat a hamburger again. In her words, she said being sued was a harrowing experience. And though it was difficult, afterwards, she went on record to say she was grateful for the experience. She learnt from it and knew she would be better for it on the other side.

I feel precisely the same way after my financial difficulties.

Rock bottom is the place most ripe for change. But we do not have to wait for rock bottom to change ourselves. Though I have earned wisdom and prosperity on the other side of my rock bottom, I do not wish rock bottom on anyone. It is possible for you to course correct before something harrowing happens in your life. You can harness the power of your mind at any point.

TECHNIQUES AND BEST PRACTICES

To make it simpler for you, I have collected all the techniques and best practices I spoke about through my journey:

- **Setting goals.** You cannot start your journey towards fulfilling your goals until you take the time to become clear: clear about your goals, intentions, and desires. Only once you know where you're going can you take steps towards that destination.
- **Consistency and focus.** Put in the daily work. Slow, progressive change will create meaningful results in your life. If you attempt to overhaul your life and find success in the short-term, you will find yourself relapsing to your old, default behaviours.
- **Defaulting to old behaviours is normal.** You do not have to

spiral back into your old ways. Take the time to physically draw a line in the air to cut the negativity out of your life. Then reaffirm your affirmations to reprogram your desired thoughts back into your mind.

- **Affirmations and visualisations.** Stay positive in your language. If you speak with negative or average language, you will invite those things into your life. I would often say, "I'm an average agent," when speaking about my career, so of course I was average!
- **Copy, copy, copy.** There is much to be learnt from the journeys and lives of other people. When you want to grow in your field, or grow as a person in any capacity, identify someone who exhibits the qualities you seek. Then copy that person. Once you copy enough, you will learn how to put your own spin on it.
- **The trilogy of success.** Be ever mindful that your thoughts, words, and actions must be in alignment to manifest meaningful results in your life.
- **Role-playing.** In and out of real estate, role-playing offers you the chance to prepare for opportunities that come your way. Like how an actor rehearses lines for a play, there is value in practising your performance for a presentation, or even a tough conversation.
- **Dress for the life you want.** Externalise the internal self you want to express to the world.

WHAT DO YOU FILL YOUR LIFE WITH?

When you undergo this journey, it will be key to examine who and what you fill your life with.

The friends you keep and family you stay in touch with inevitably influence you. Depending how much time you spend with them will determine how much influence they have on your concepts and beliefs. You must be intentional about who you spend time with. It can be especially dangerous if you spend extended time with "complainers" or any negative-minded people. A large part of why I told no one about my Three Month Experiment was because I didn't want anyone's judgments or opinions to derail me from my goal.

Scientists have created a term for how our inner dialogue and belief systems shape us: it's called neuro-linguistic programming. In essence, it speaks to how our inner stories, social media, and social circle influence our behaviour and actions. That is why it is key to fill your life with positive messaging and positive influences. You will be barraged by these messages. Depending on what you listen to and who you spend time with, they will leave an imprint on you, good or bad.

Identify role models in your life. Find positive people who inspire feelings of goodness, kindness, or courage in you. Seek out mentors and friends who provide value to your life, and you should seek to provide value in return.

Do not underestimate the power of the other experiences and items that fill your life as well. For example, books are powerful, and they enter your life when you most need it. A book is one of the best ways to accelerate change in your life—after all, a book is a journey someone else has already been on. They have simply recounted the journey for you.

I used books to accelerate change in my life. *Mind Power, Think and Grow Rich,* and *The Master Key to Riches* were vital guideposts through my journey. Each book helped me take my work to the next level.

You do not have to have an in-depth understanding of your path, and you do not have to forge out on a new path you have created. You can follow the paths of those who came before you until you find your path.

START WHERE YOU ARE

If you're like me, it can be difficult to get out of your funk if you haven't been exposed to positive influences like this work or very successful people. It is easy for you to keep walking the path you have always walked and wonder why your life isn't changing.

However, everything is right there for the taking.

You can have the life you want.

You can have the life you secretly dream about.

You just have to open the door to change and capitalise on the strategies and techniques I've laid out in this book. I've given you the groundwork and understanding you need to begin your journey.

But first, you have to acknowledge that you may not be living the life you want. You have to see where you are so you can start from where you are. Then decide where you want to go and how you're going to get there. When you decide your first goal, do not try to bite off more than you can chew. Do not set yourself up for failure. You want an ambitious but reasonable goal that you can achieve within three months.

And then one day, you may well be where you've always wanted to be.

Acknowledgements

My first debt of gratitude goes to Barfoot & Thompson. This incredible company has not only given me a platform for success in real estate, but it has also shaped my life in so many respects. I have met incredible people through my days of selling real estate, I have worked with amazing teams in my role as Branch Manager, and through this company I have been given the opportunity to provide an incredible life for my family. I also give a special shout out of thanks to Tracey Boyle, Els de Jong, and all of my team at City Branch—they are simply some of the best in the business, and I am nothing without them. I would like to thank the Directors of this company: Peter Thompson, Stephen Barfoot, Kiri Barfoot, and Garth Barfoot (now retired) for your belief in me. I would also like to thank Chris Dobbie, our CEO, for his patience and faith in me. This book has been written for Barfoot & Thompson as a gesture of appreciation so that anyone in this business who is just starting, or anyone who needs to reset, can get some guidance from someone who has already walked the highs and lows before them.

I would like to also thank Ian Gray (now retired), my Barfoot &

Thompson Branch Manager at Mt Eden Branch. He built a legacy in our company and is quite simply one of the most important people in my real estate career. He never put himself first—it was always about the team or what he could do to help you in your career. A legend.

I would also like to thank John Kehoe and Napoleon Hill—two men who wrote books that changed my life.

I would also like to thank the team at Scribe Media—especially Janice Bashman. She has helped me formulate my draft writing, thoughts, and concepts into a book that sounds like me and reads like me. She kept me on track when I was going off on tangents and has helped me to create a book I am proud of. Thank you, Janice—I am looking forward to meeting you when you get down under to New Zealand.

And finally, I would like to gratefully acknowledge the love and support from my family. My husband, Dave, and my kids, Ruby, Nick, and Lily. They have kept me inspired to always try to show what is possible. Anyone who knows me knows how important my family is to me, especially my kids. They are without a doubt the most important thing in my life. I love them, and I am so proud of them all.

CPSIA information can be obtained
at www.ICGtesting.com
Printed in the USA
BVHW040245130223
658285BV00002B/454

9 781544 538969